# MEDITATION
## COLORING BOOK

# MEDITATION
## COLORING BOOK
### Wonderful images to melt your worries away

CHARTWELL
BOOKS

This edition printed in 2015 by
CHARTWELL BOOKS
an imprint of Book Sales
a division of Quarto Publishing Group USA Inc.
142 West 36th Street, 4th Floor
New York, New York 10018

Copyright © Arcturus Holdings Limited
26/27 Bickels Yard, 151–153 Bermondsey Street,
London SE1 3HA

ISBN: 978-0-7858-3287-4
AD004597NT

Printed in China
Reprinted 2015 (three times).

# Introduction

Coloring is a useful relaxation technique which helps you enter a freer state of being. *The Meditation Coloring Book* contains a mass of mandalas and other abstract images to soothe the mind and please the senses. It is designed to take you to that peaceful place where meditation can occur.

Mandalas are 'sacred circles', geometric shapes without a beginning or an end. They echo the balance and symmetry of the world around us – from the nucleus of a cell to the structure of a snowflake – and they symbolize harmony, wholeness and healing.

By coloring in these designs you will de-stress your mind and body and create your own beautiful artwork. So put your worries on hold, pick up your crayons, pencils or felt-tips, and let zen be your guide . . .

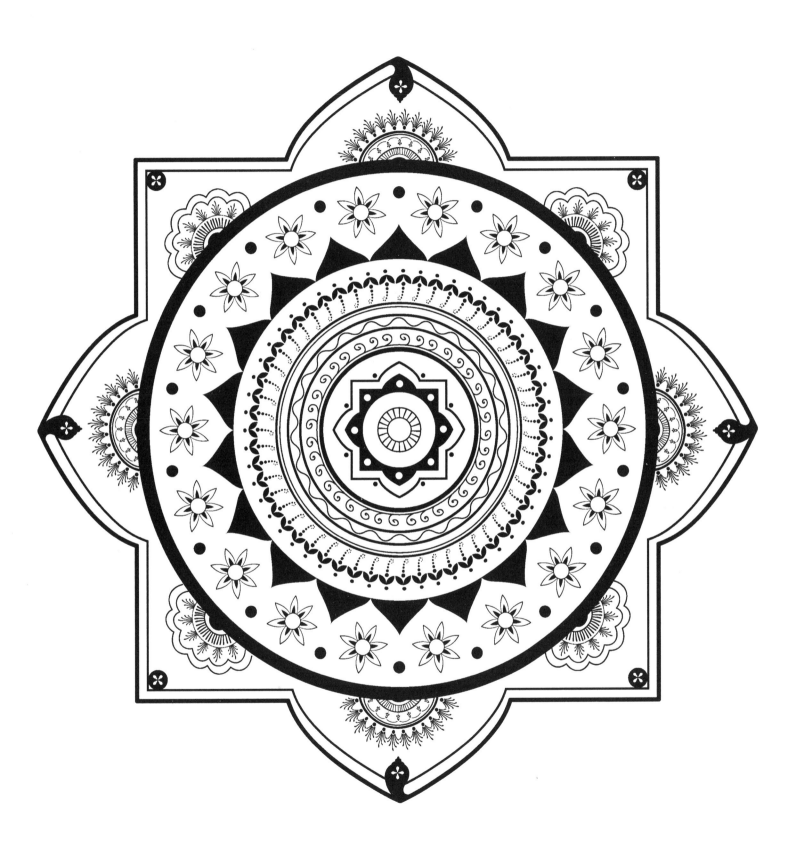

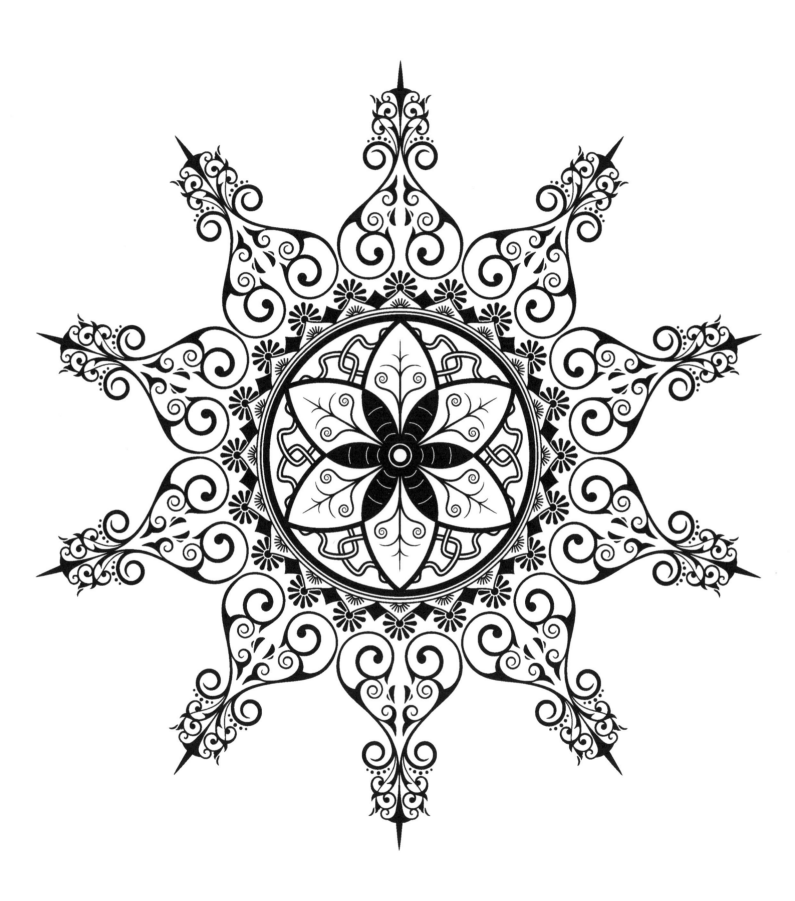

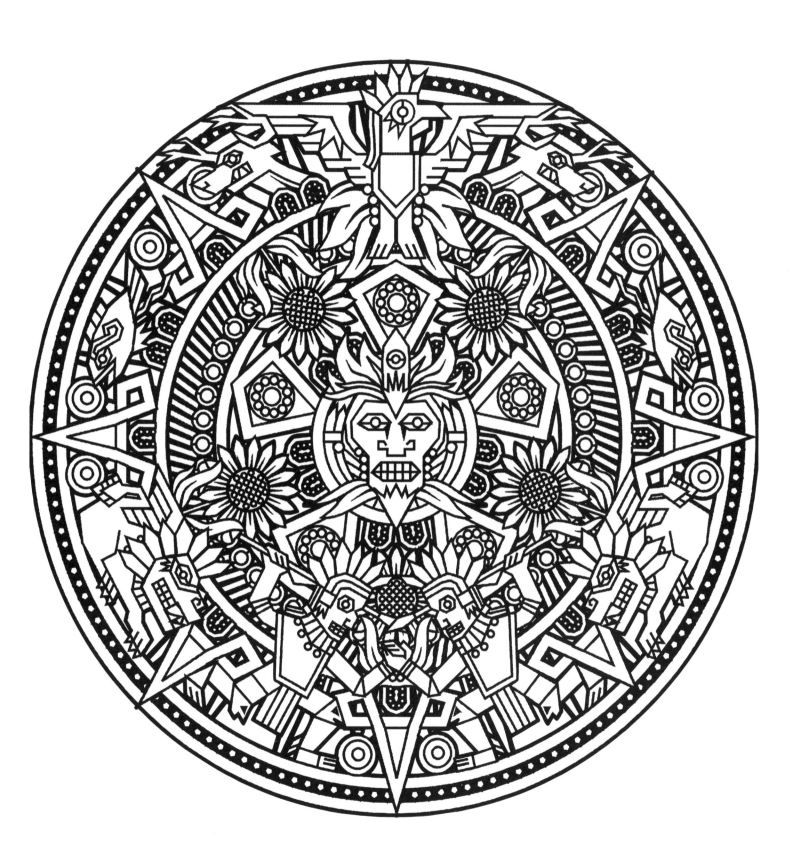

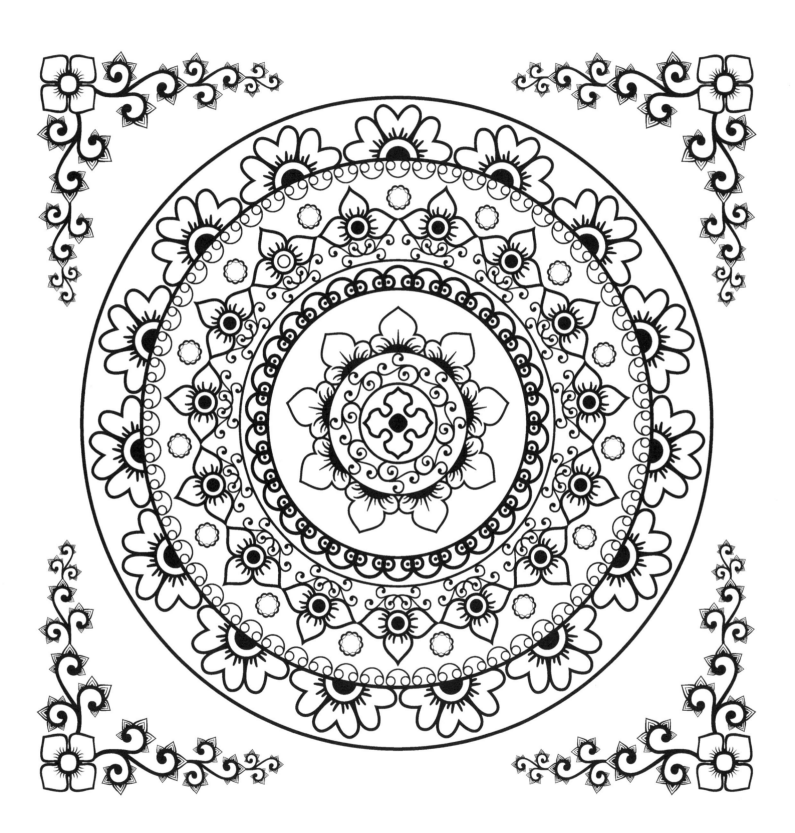

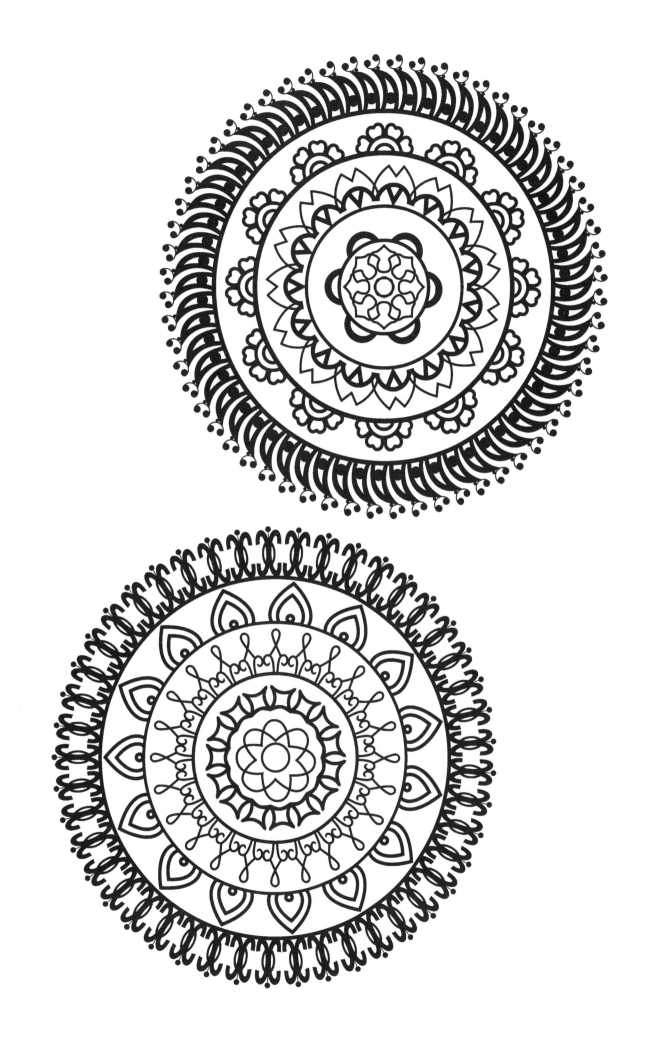

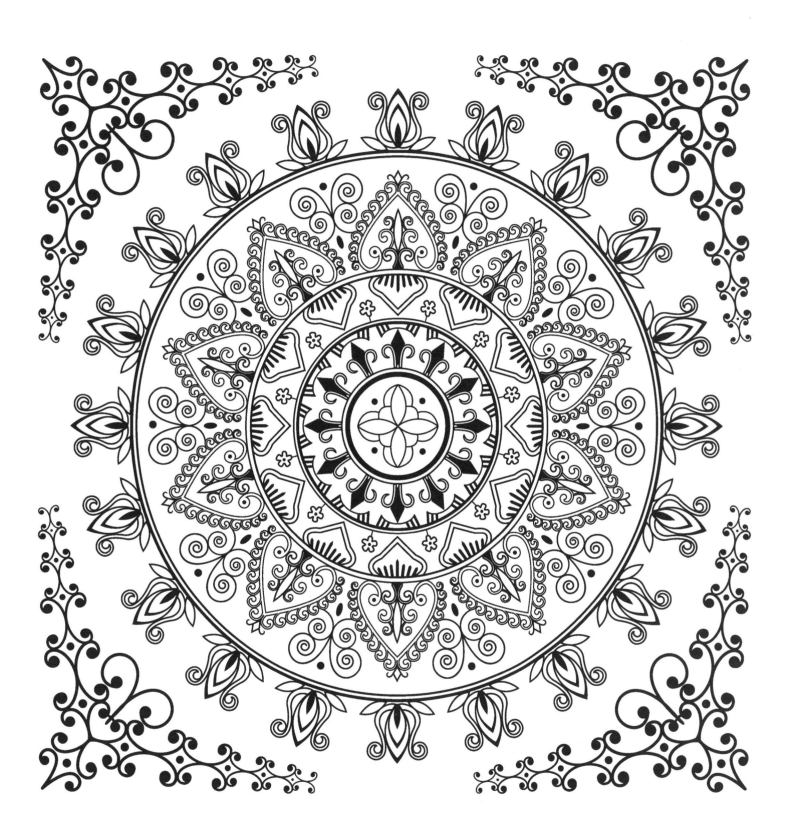

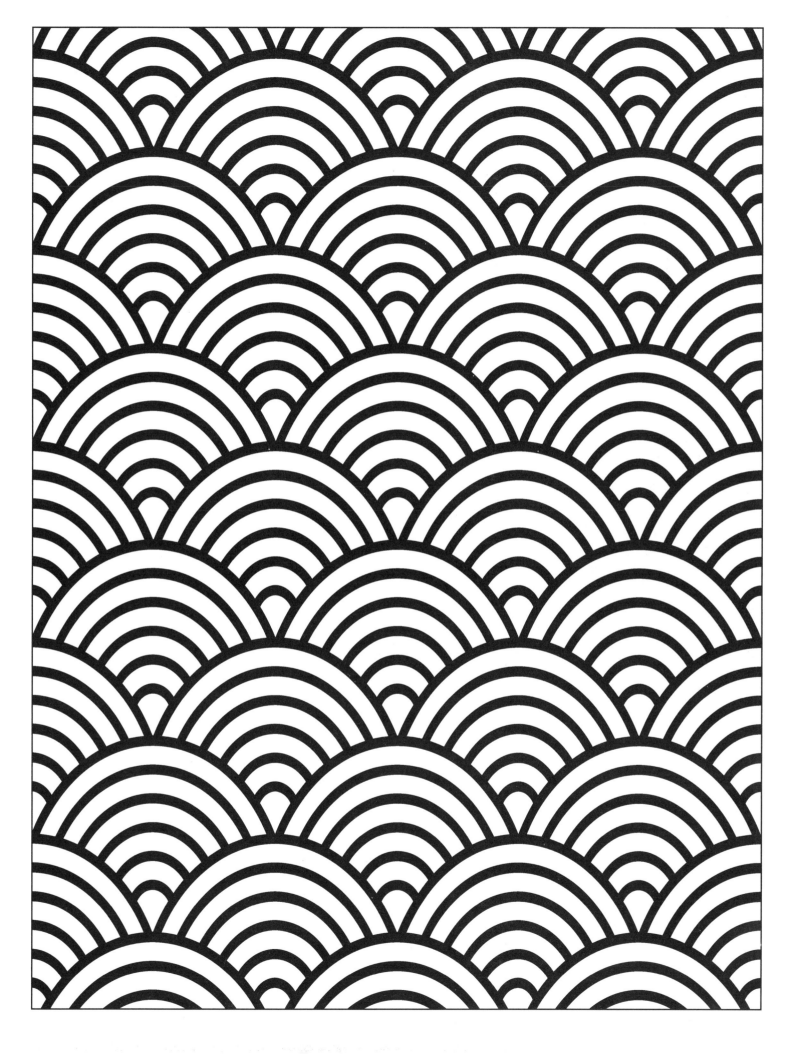

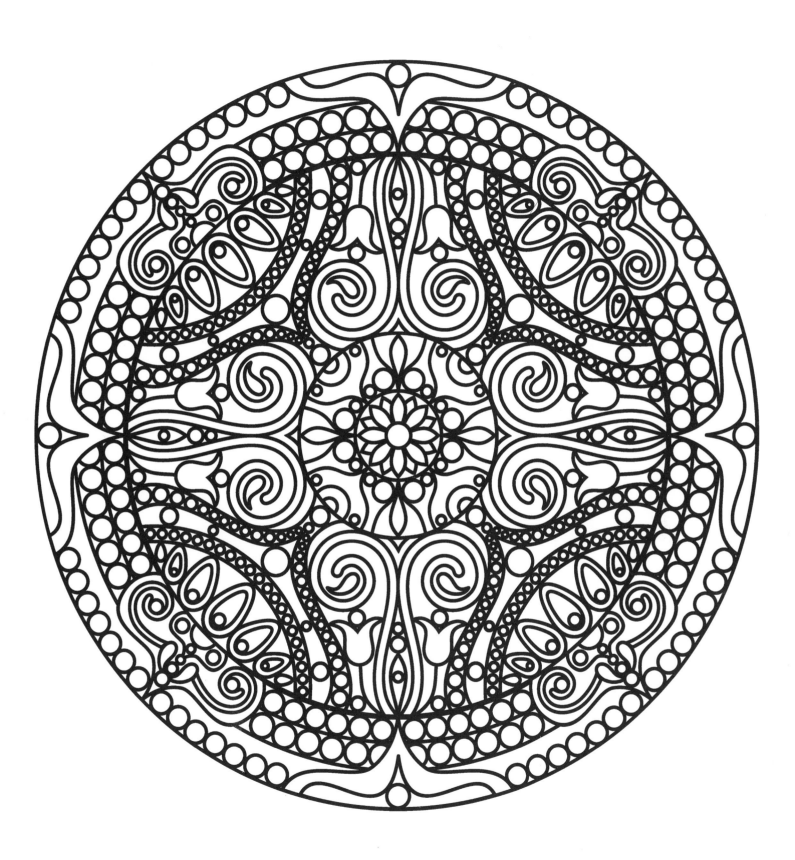

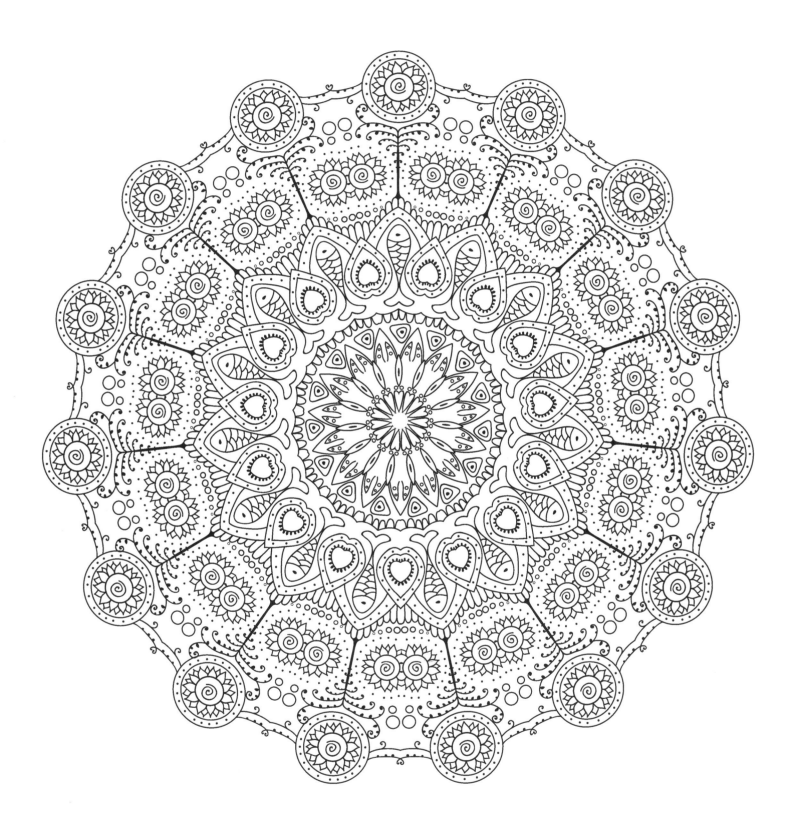

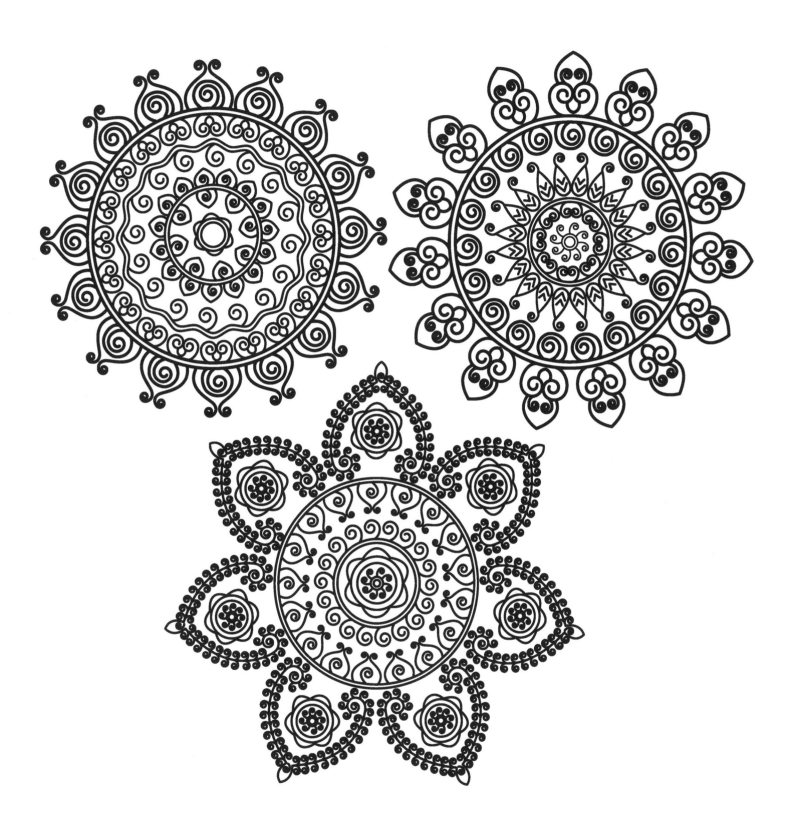

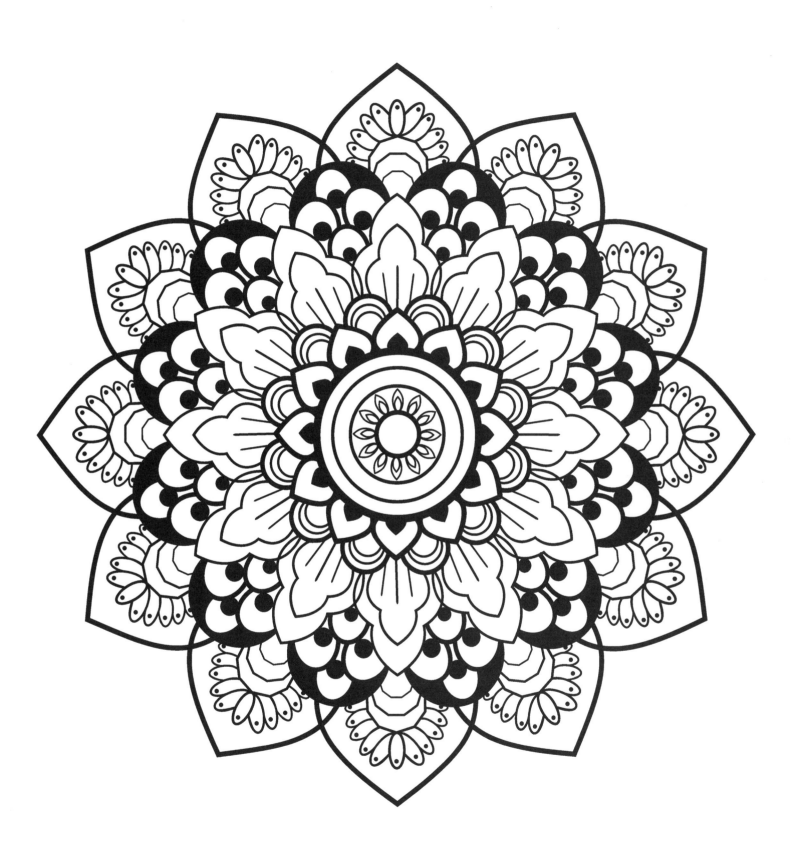

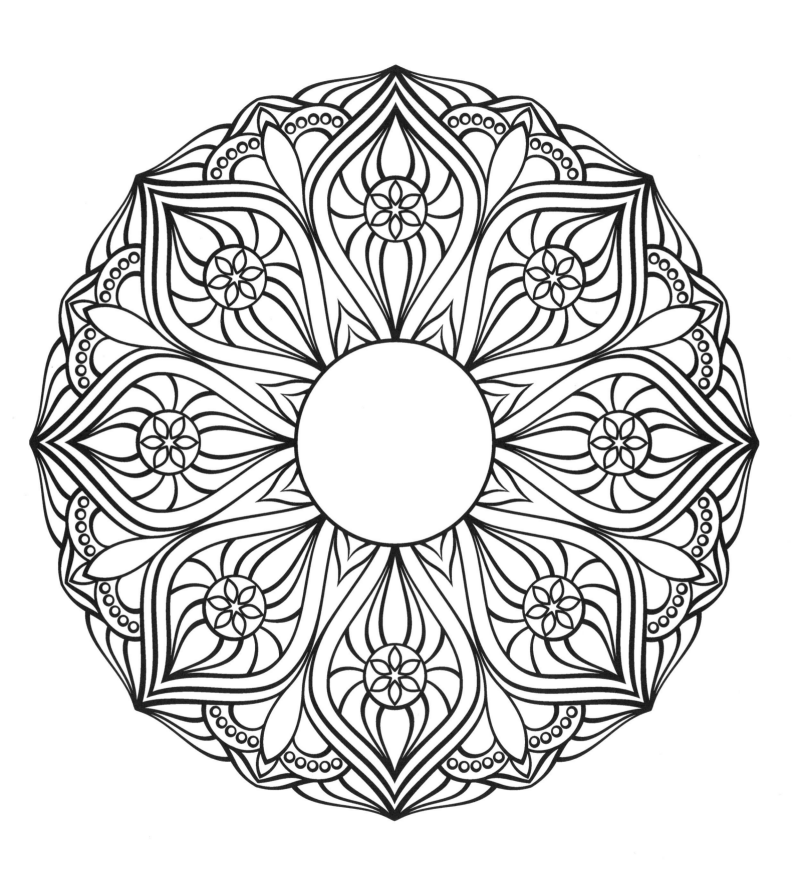

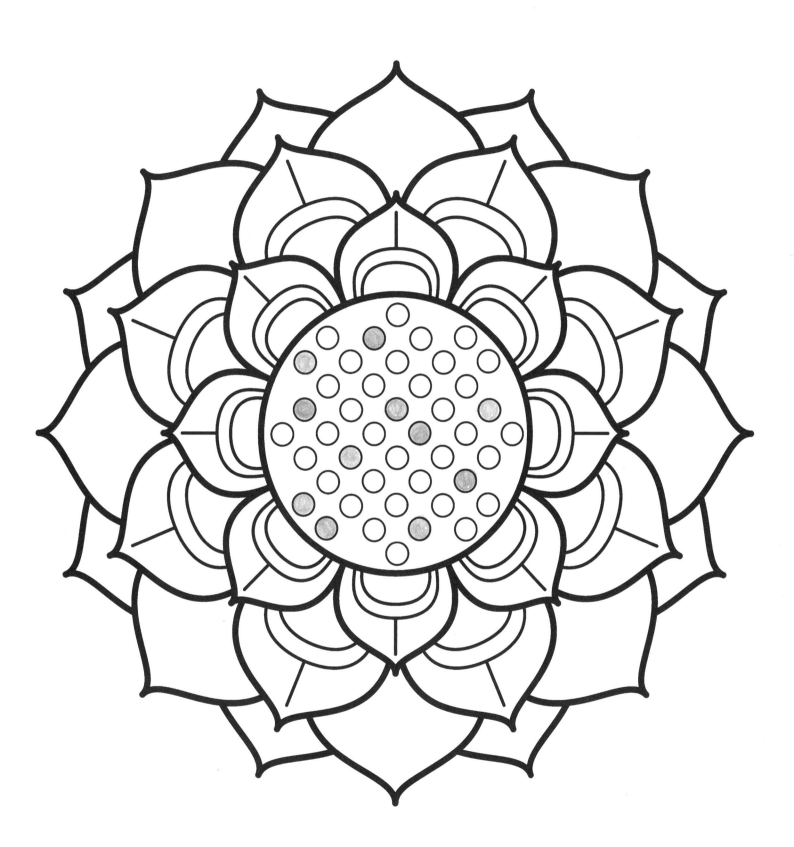

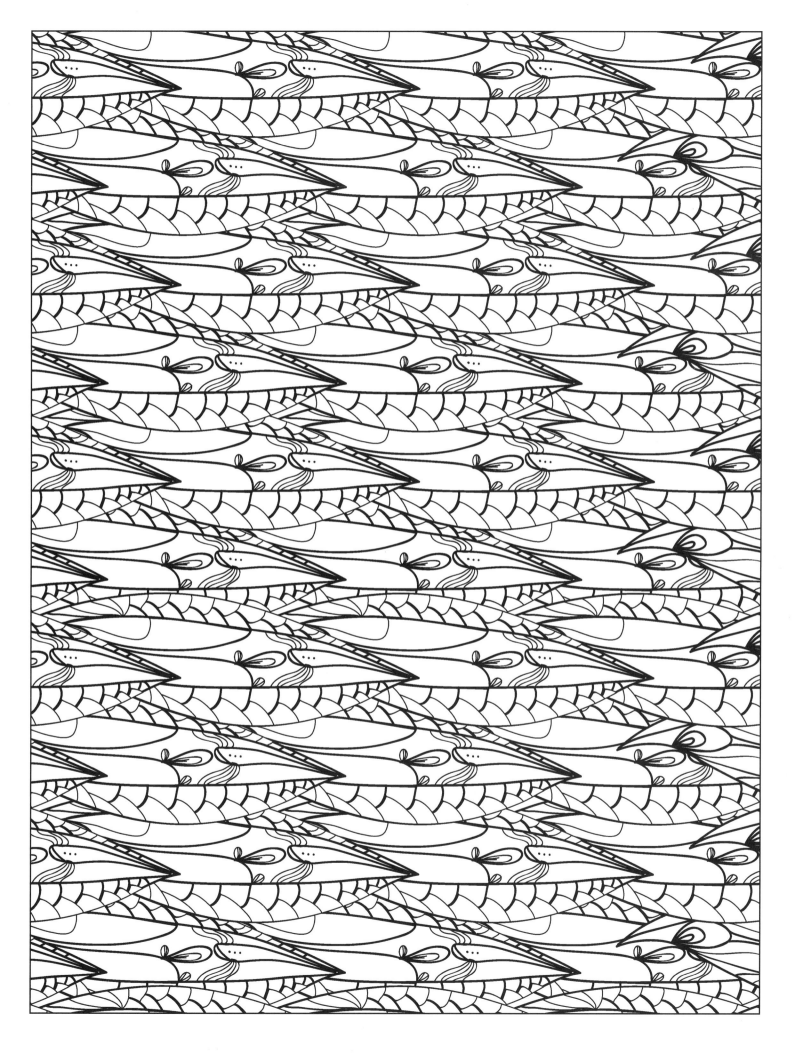

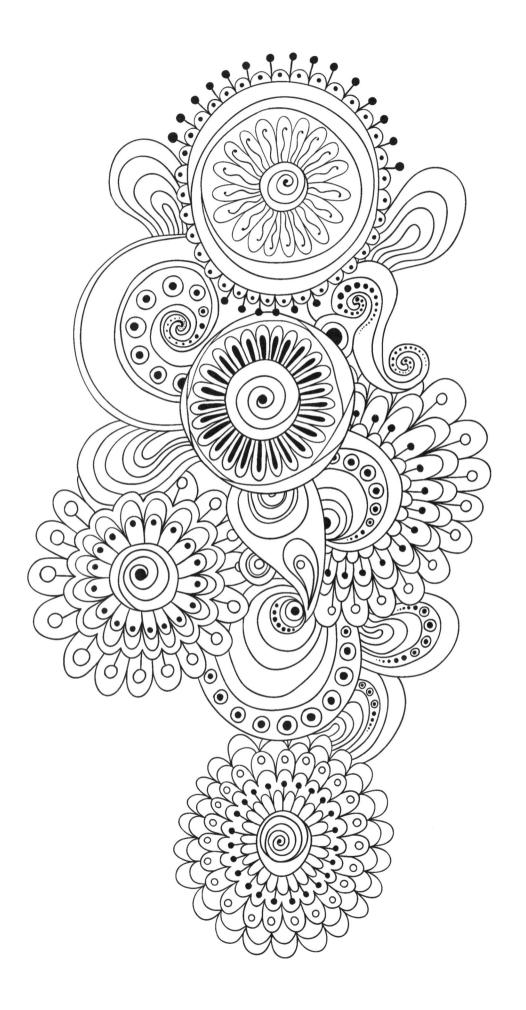

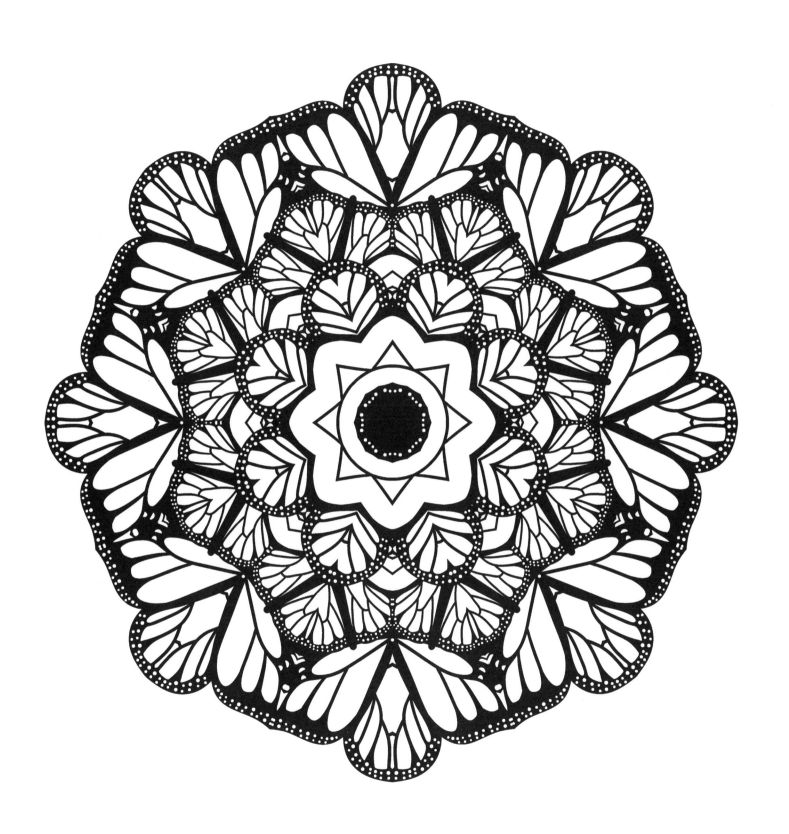

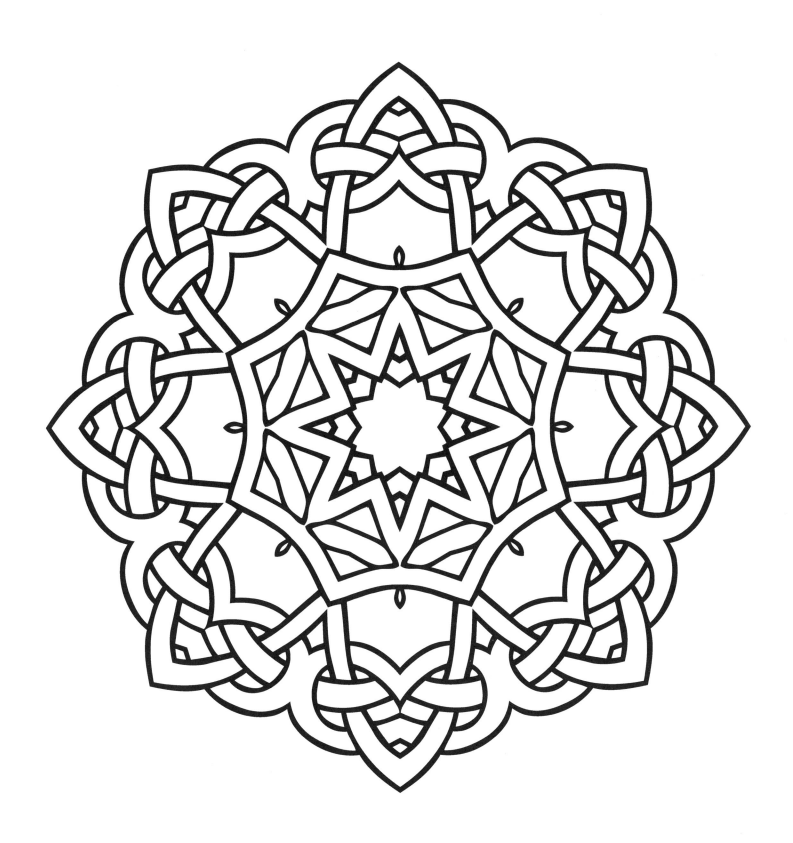

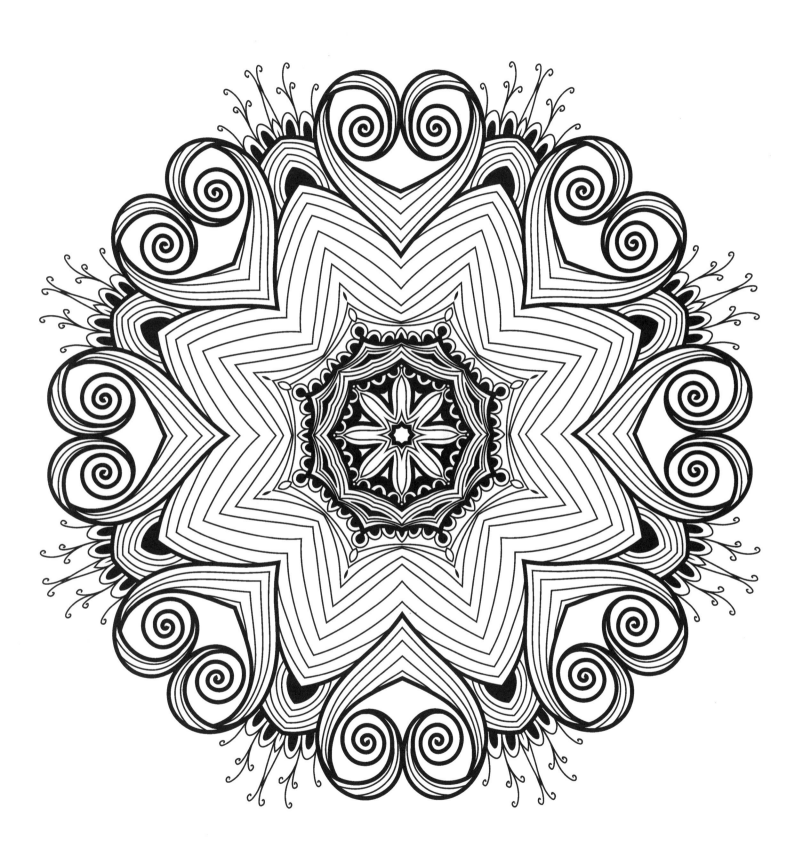

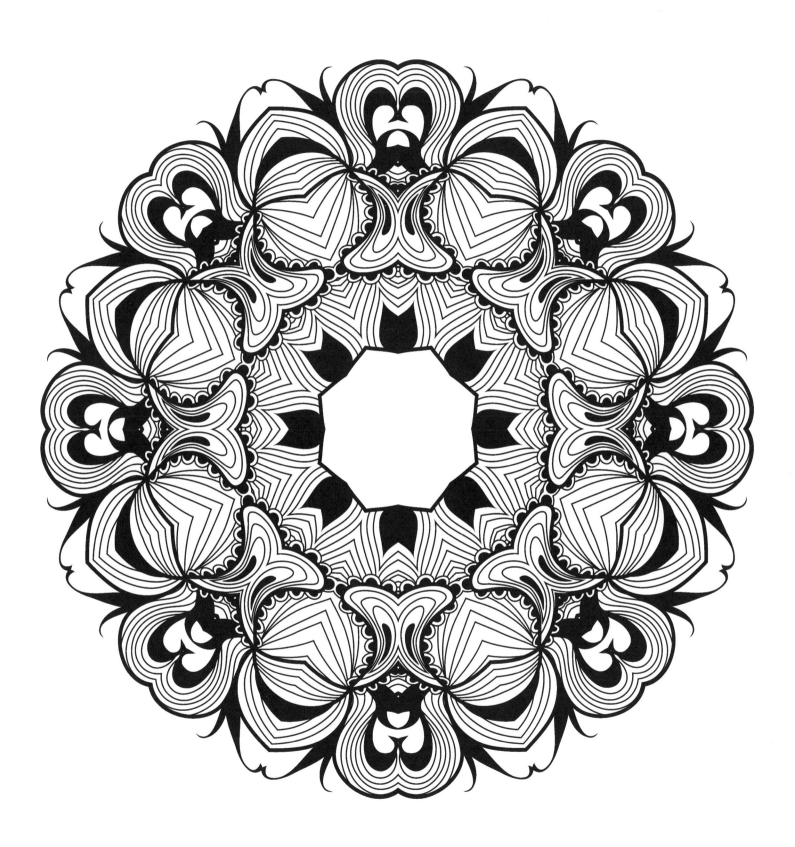

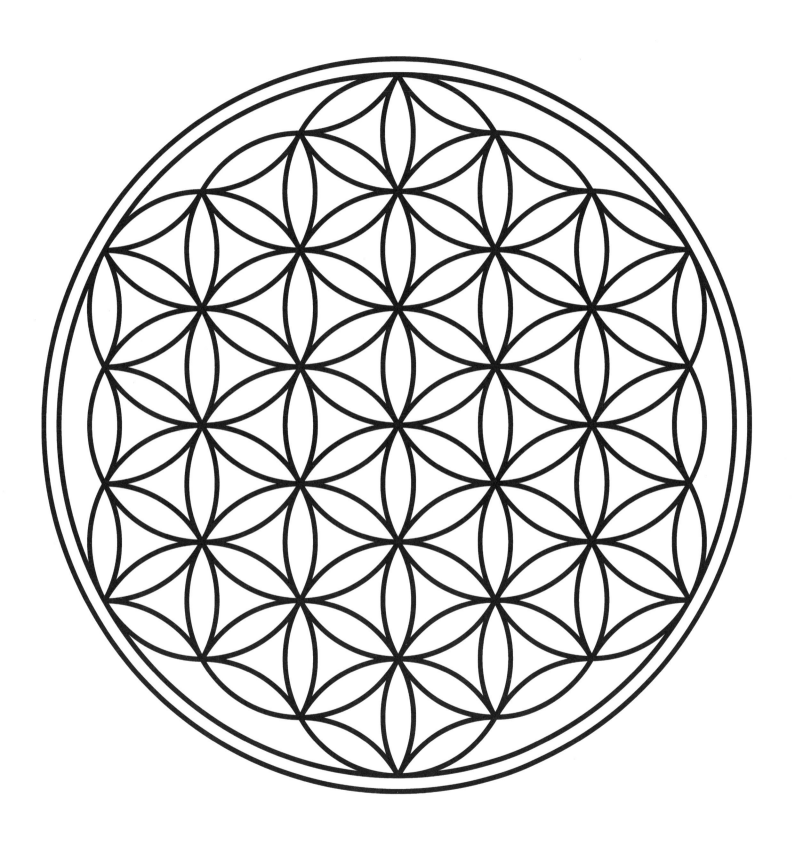

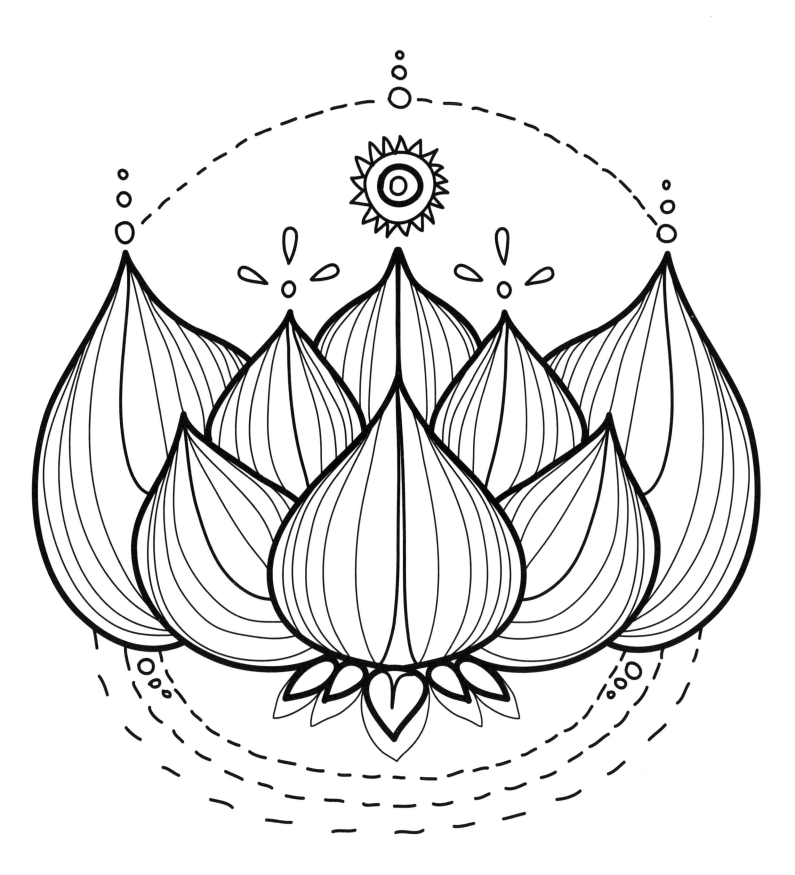

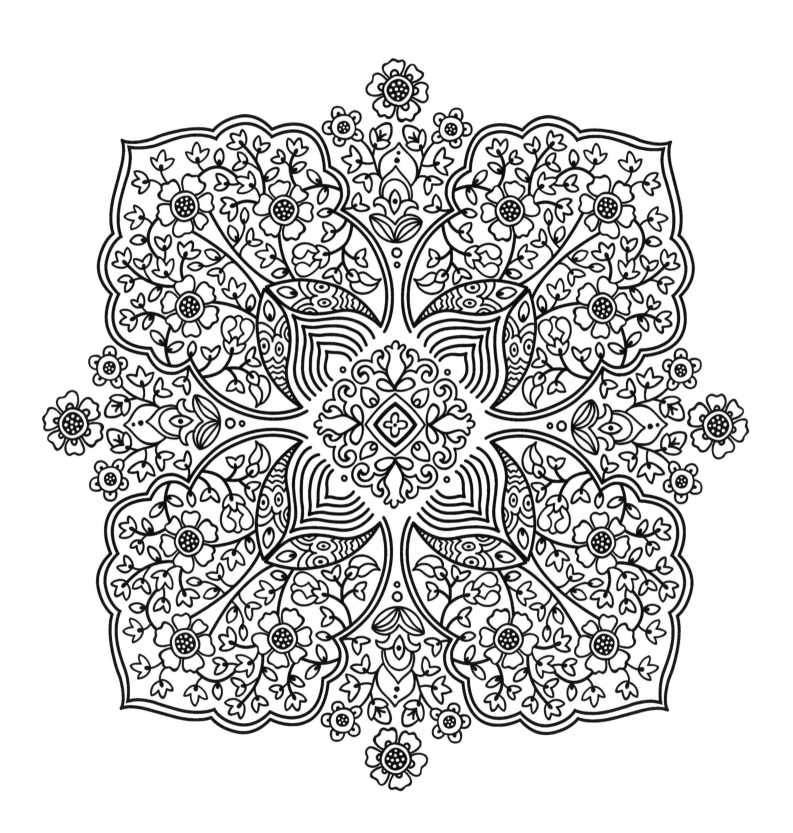

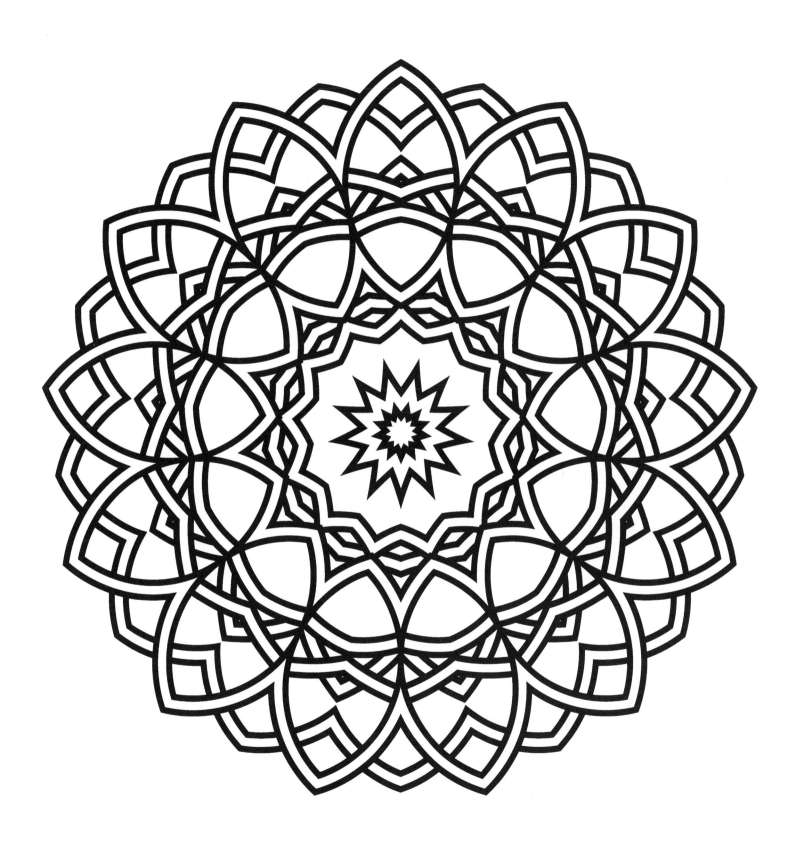

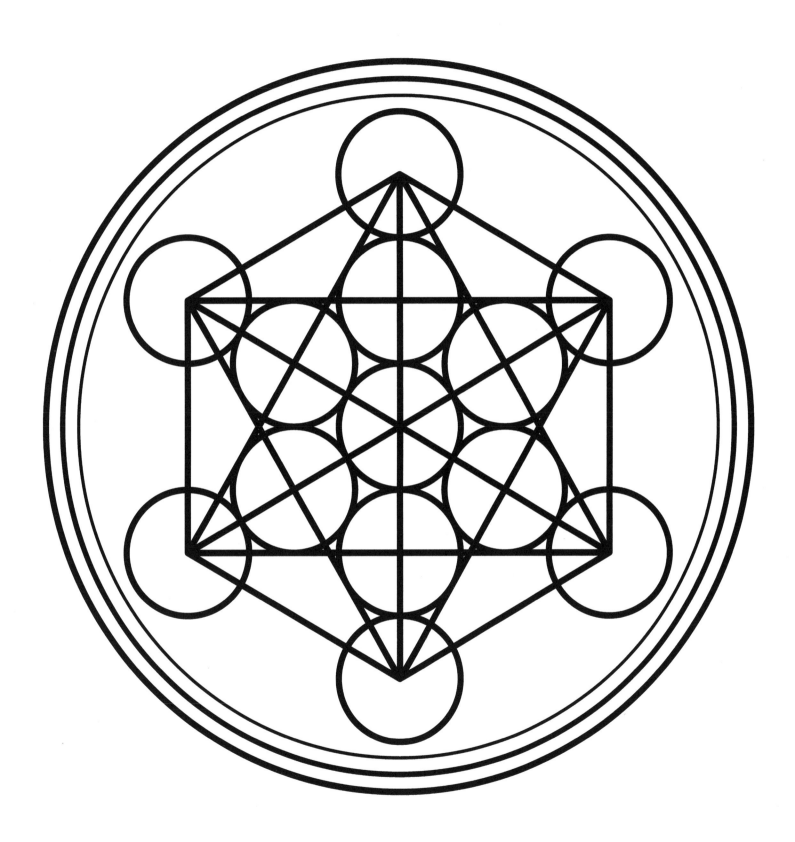

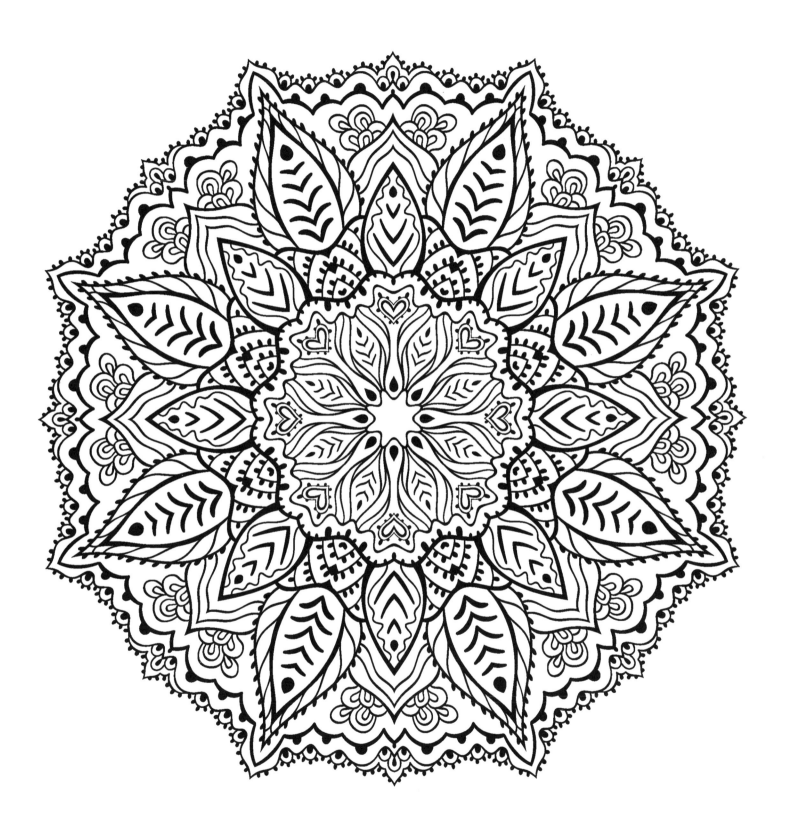

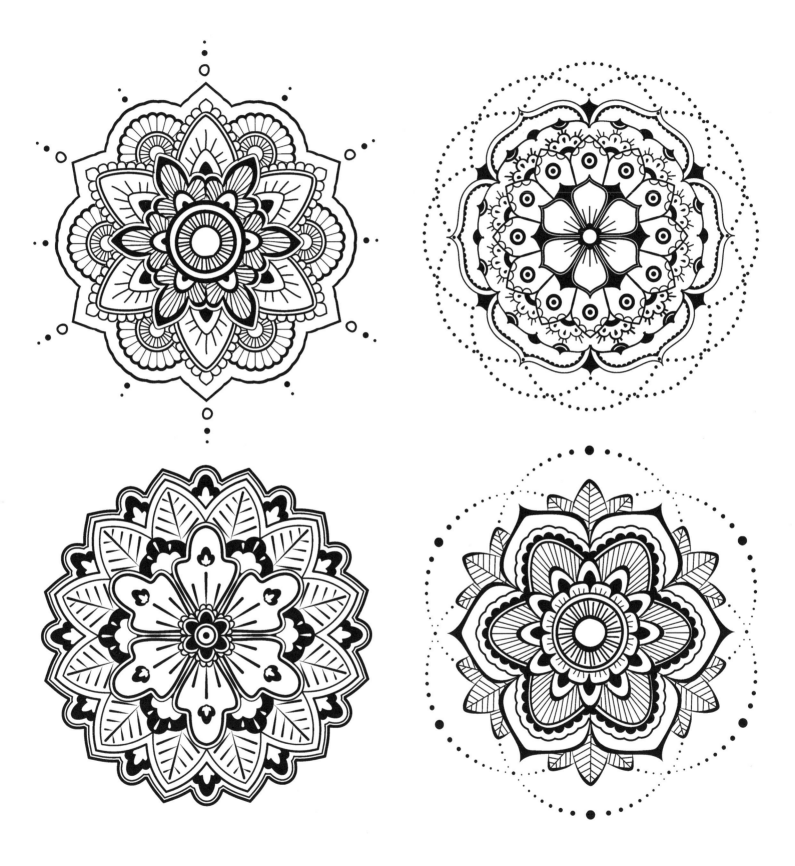

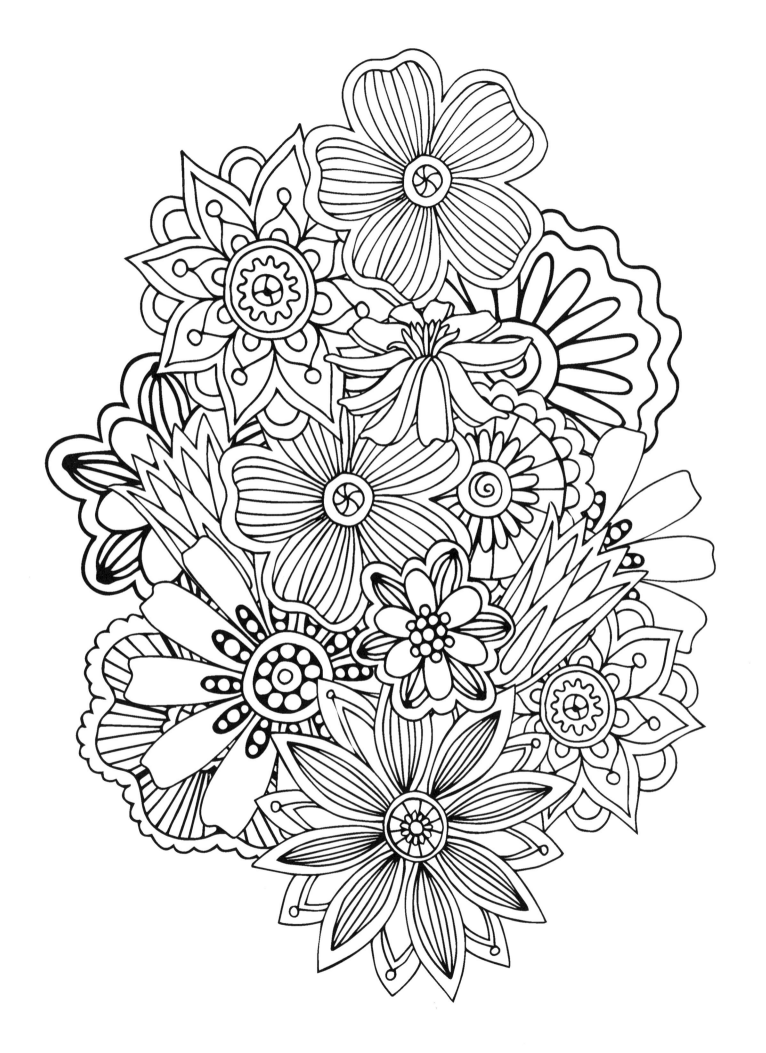

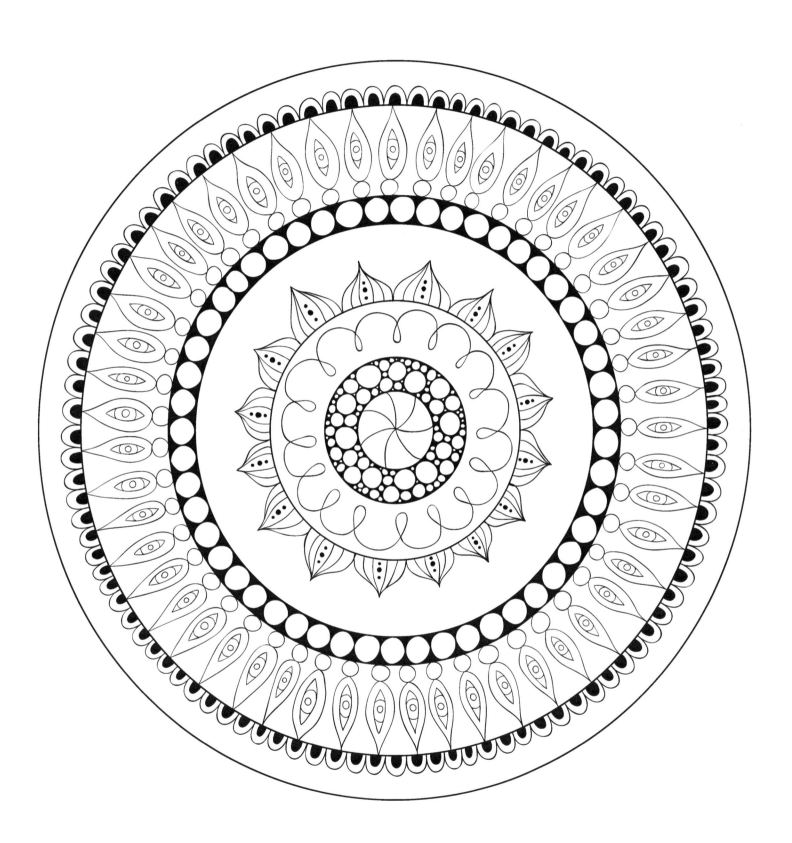

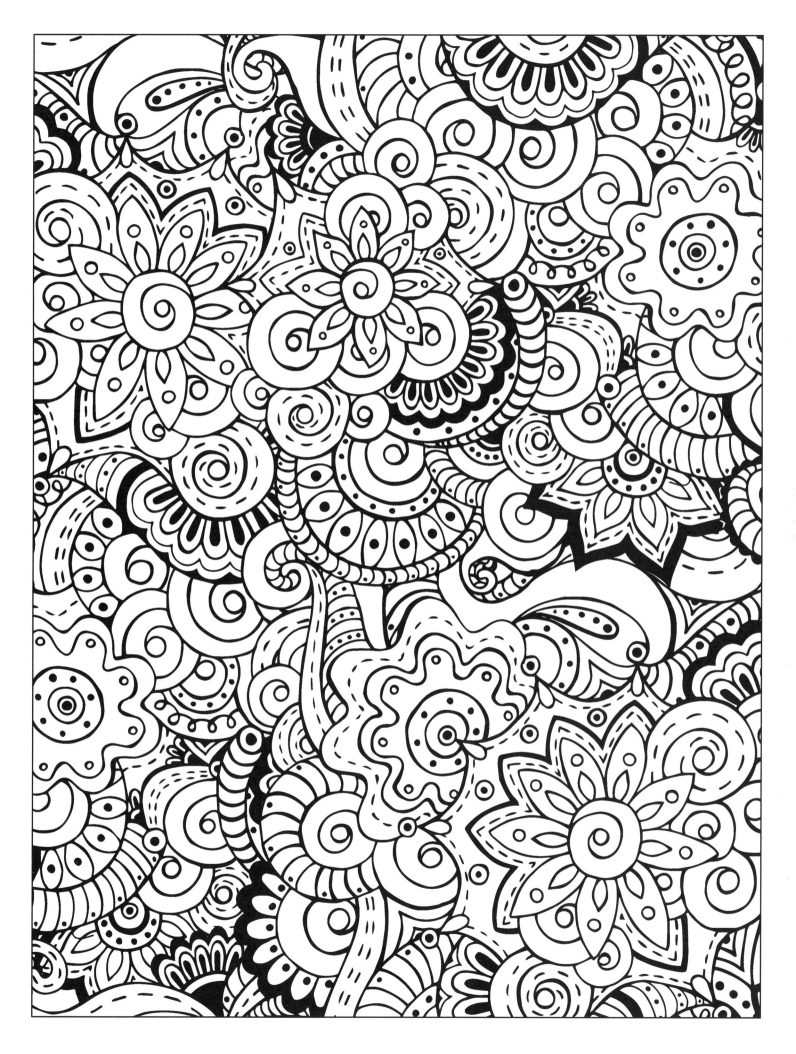

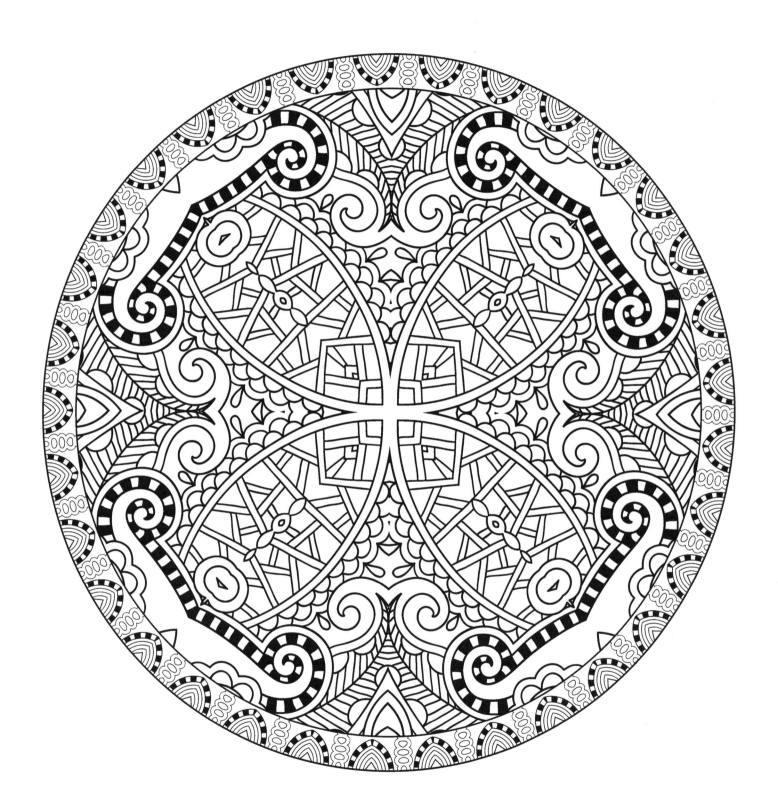

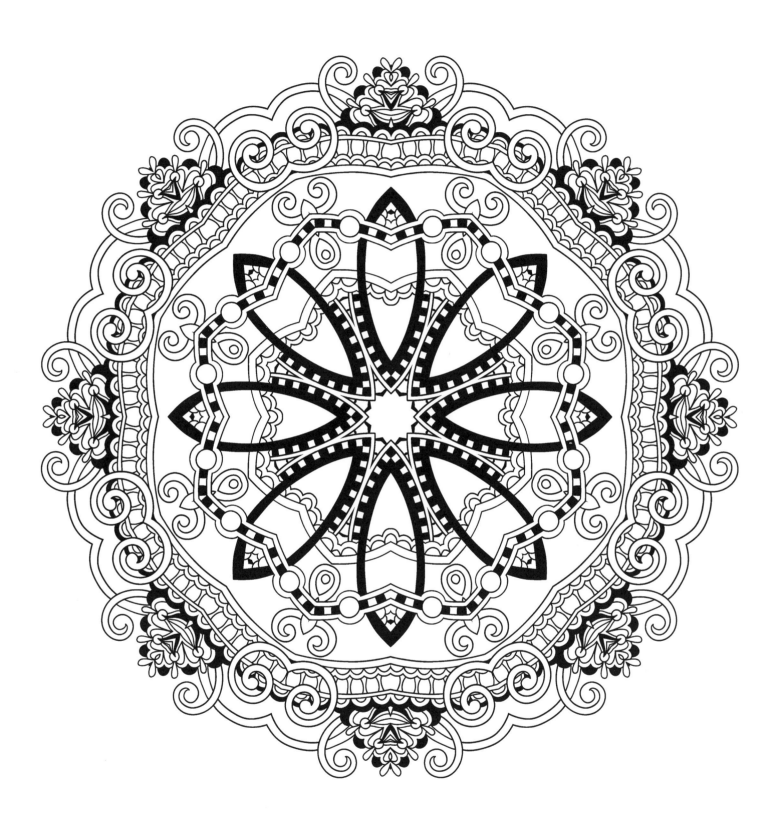

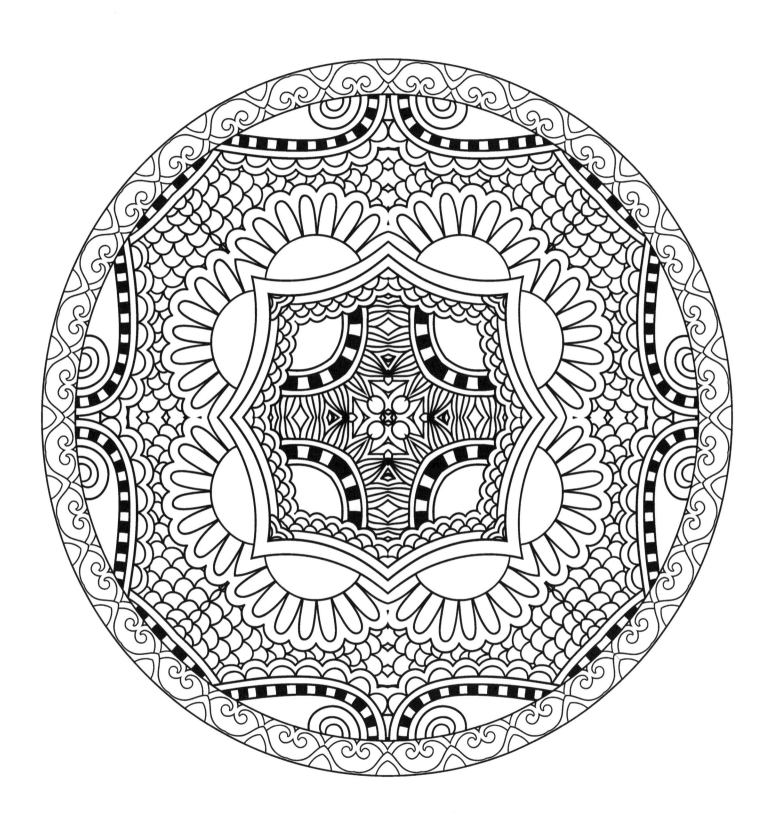

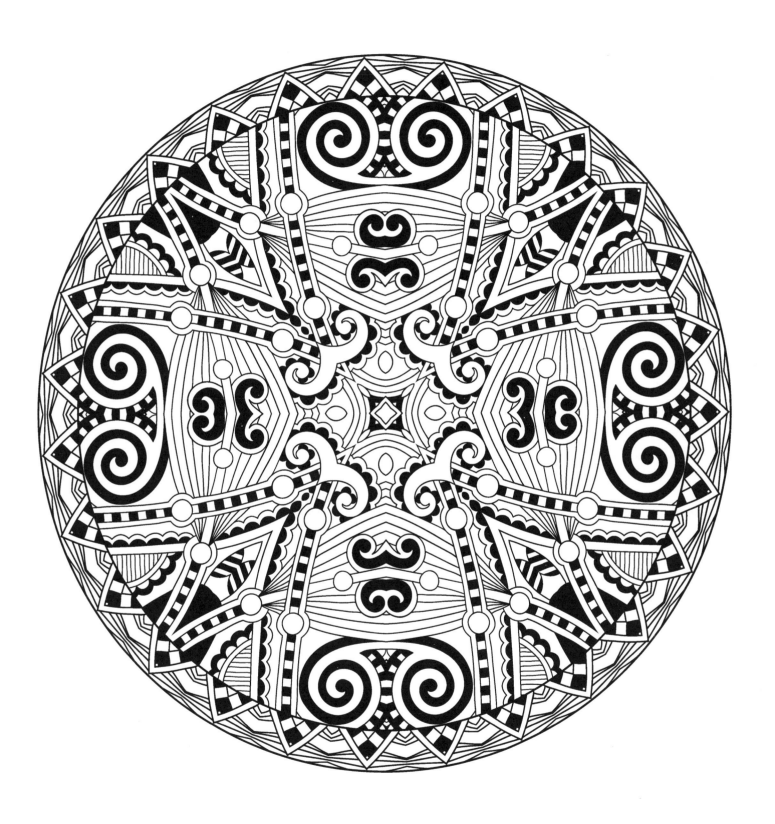

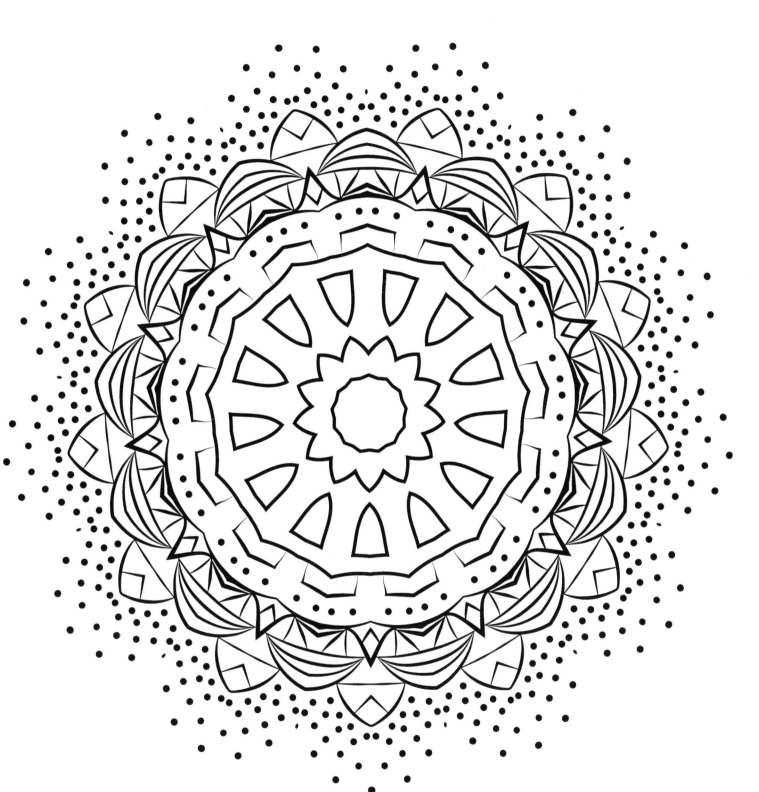

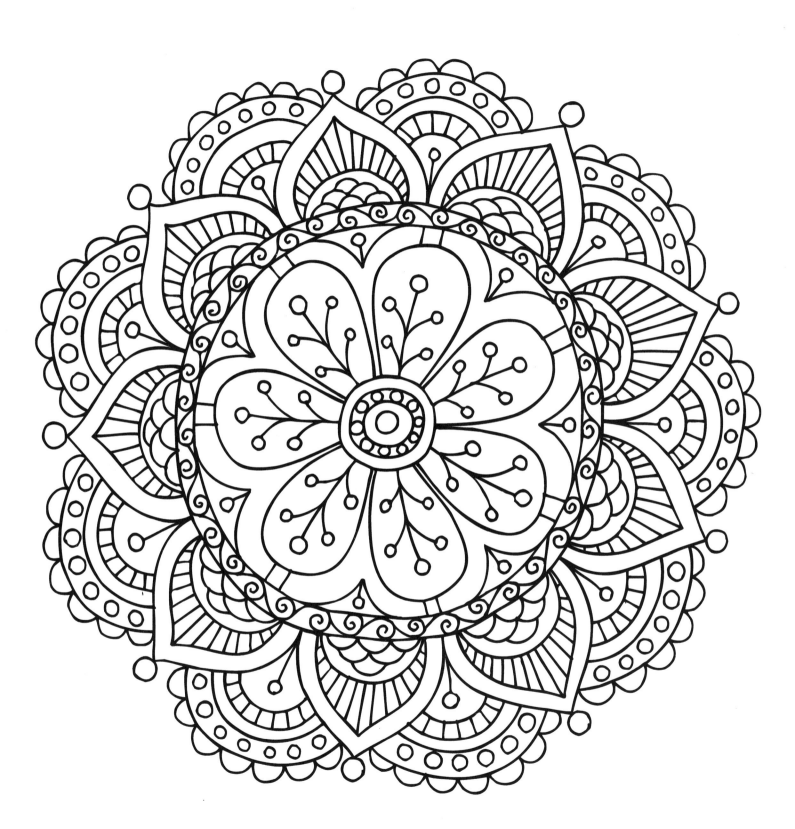

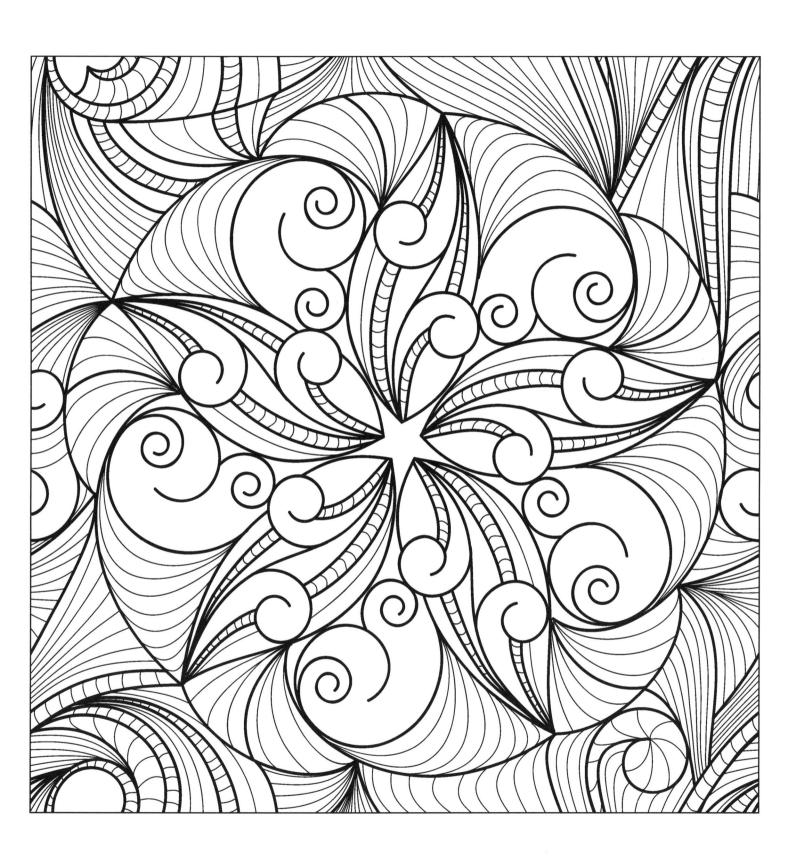

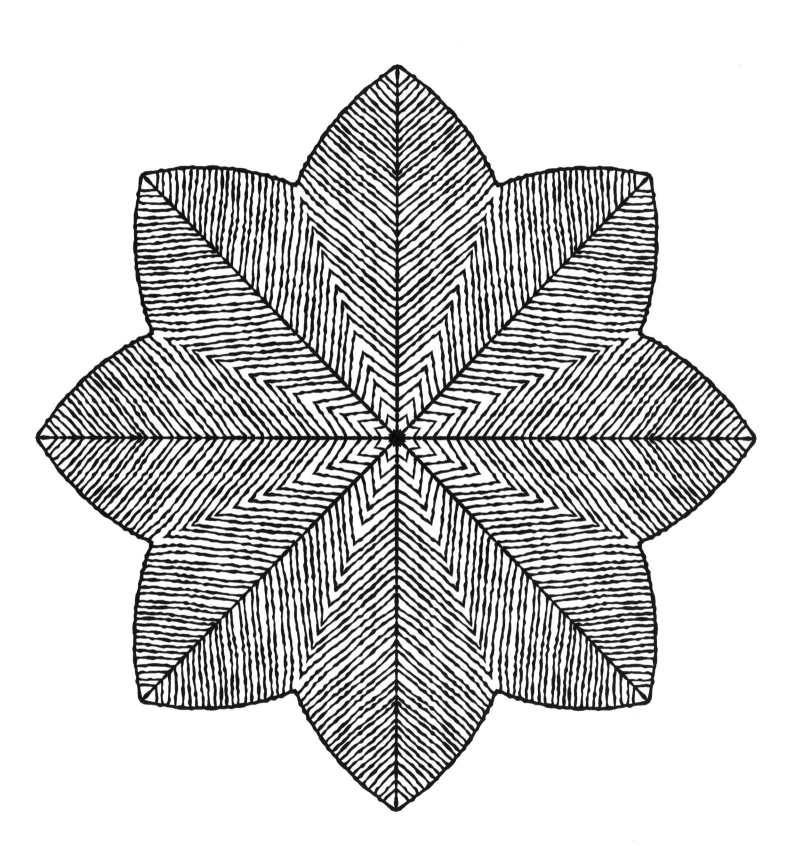

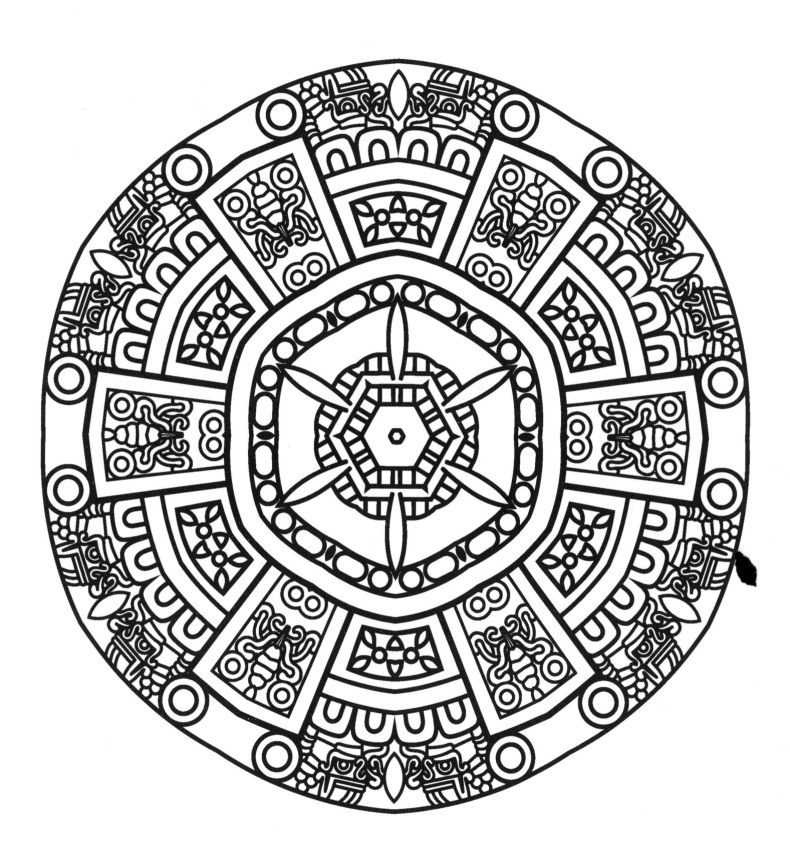

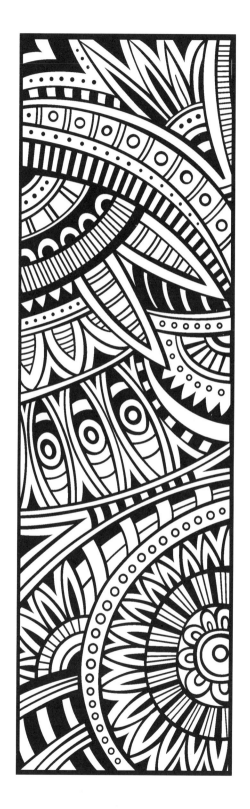
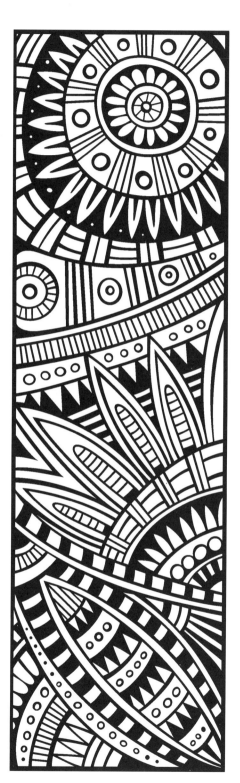
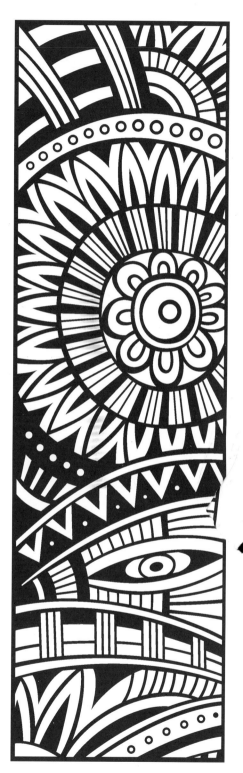

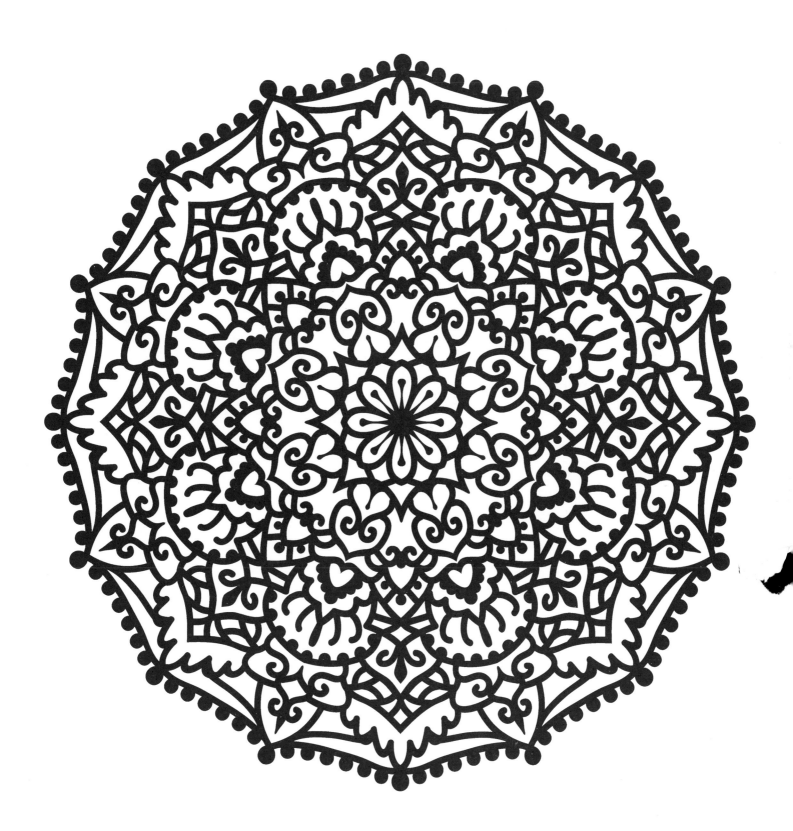

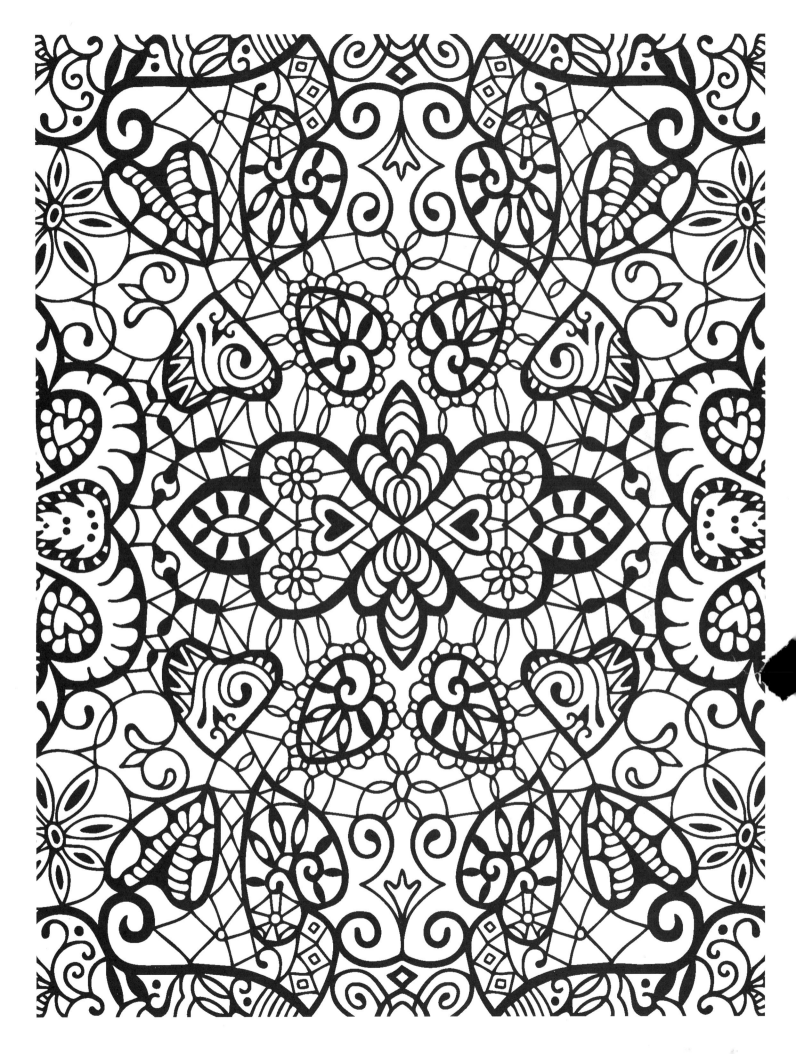

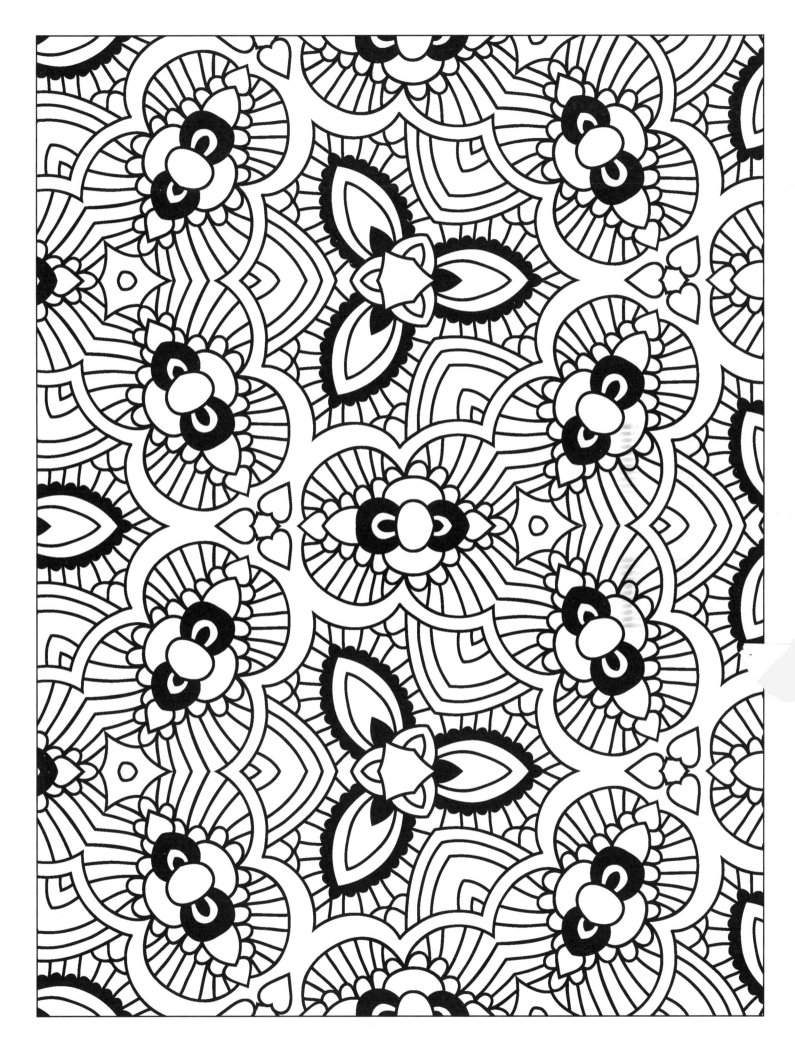

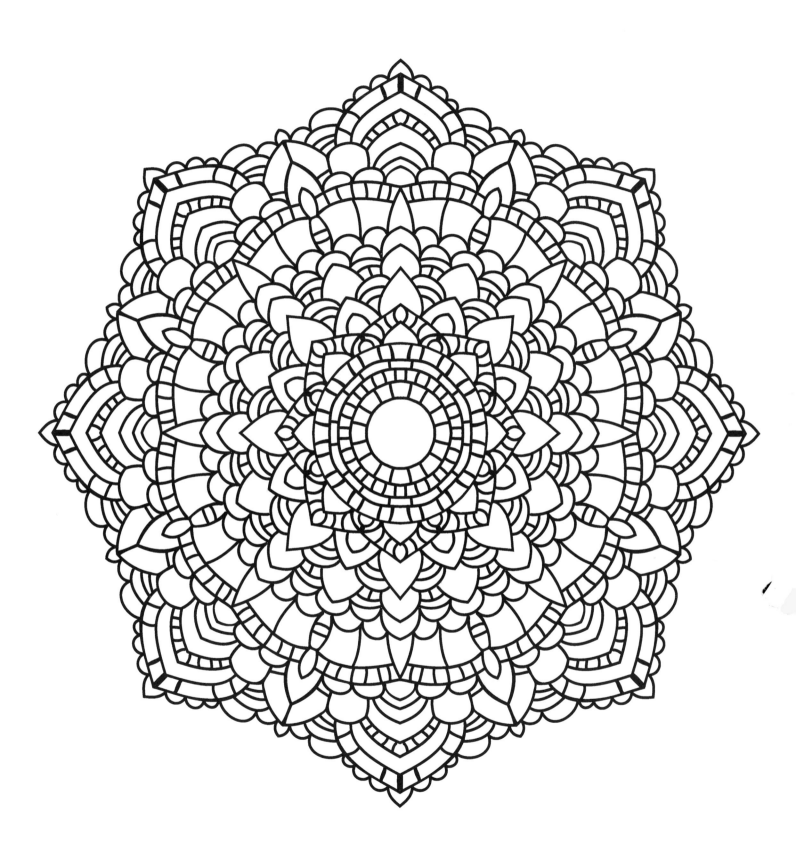

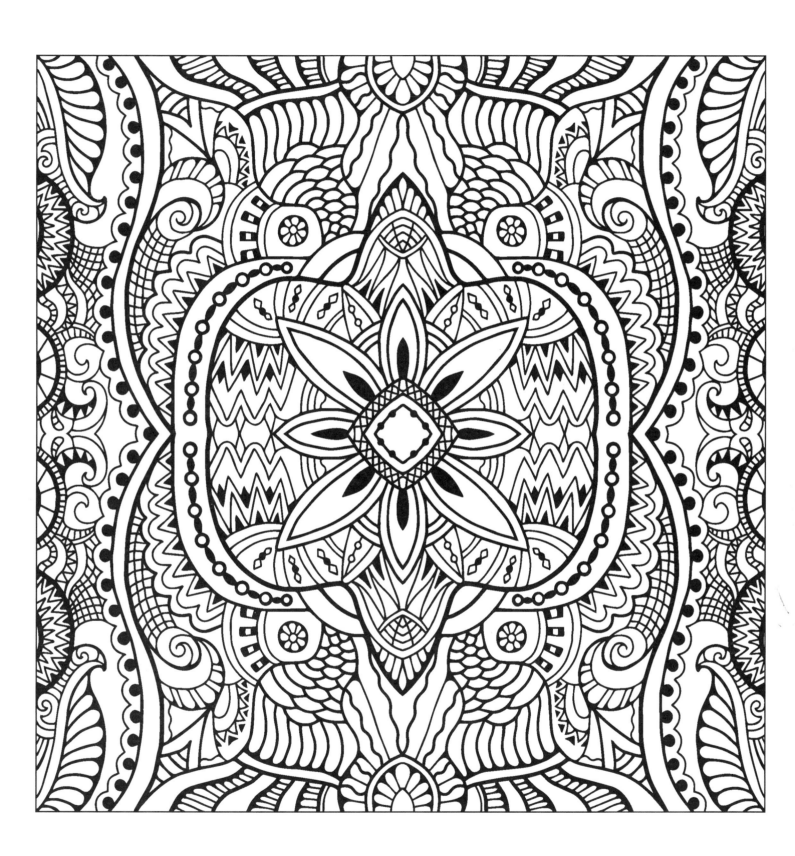

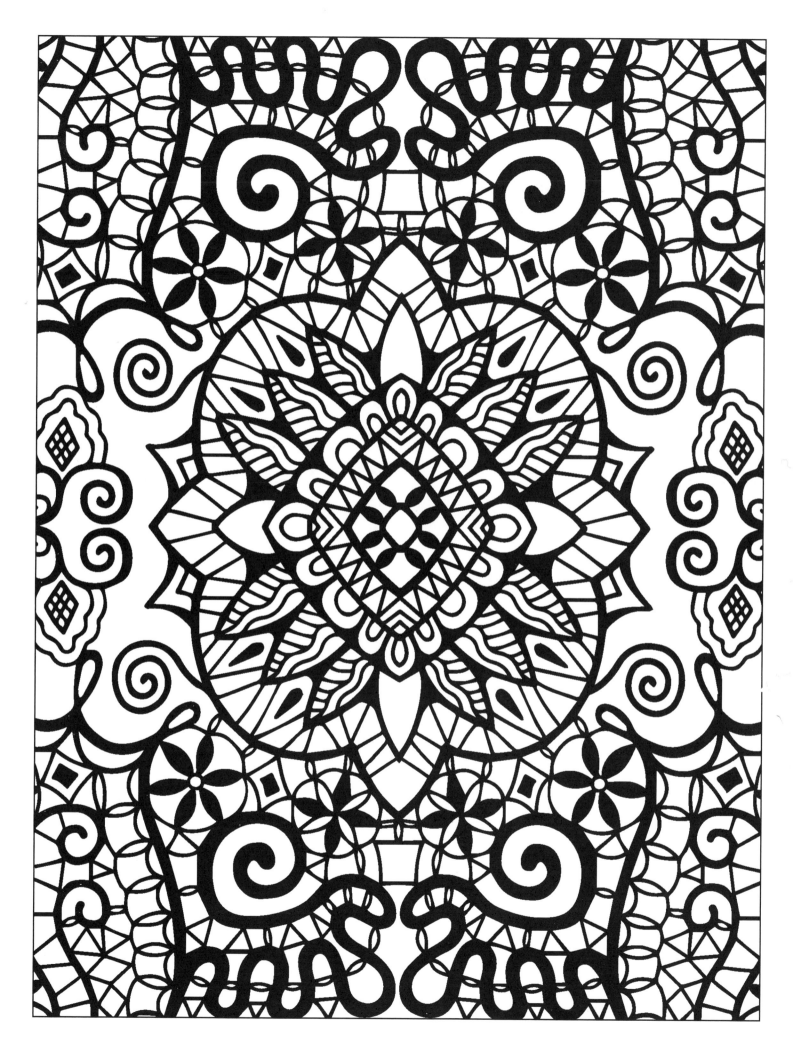

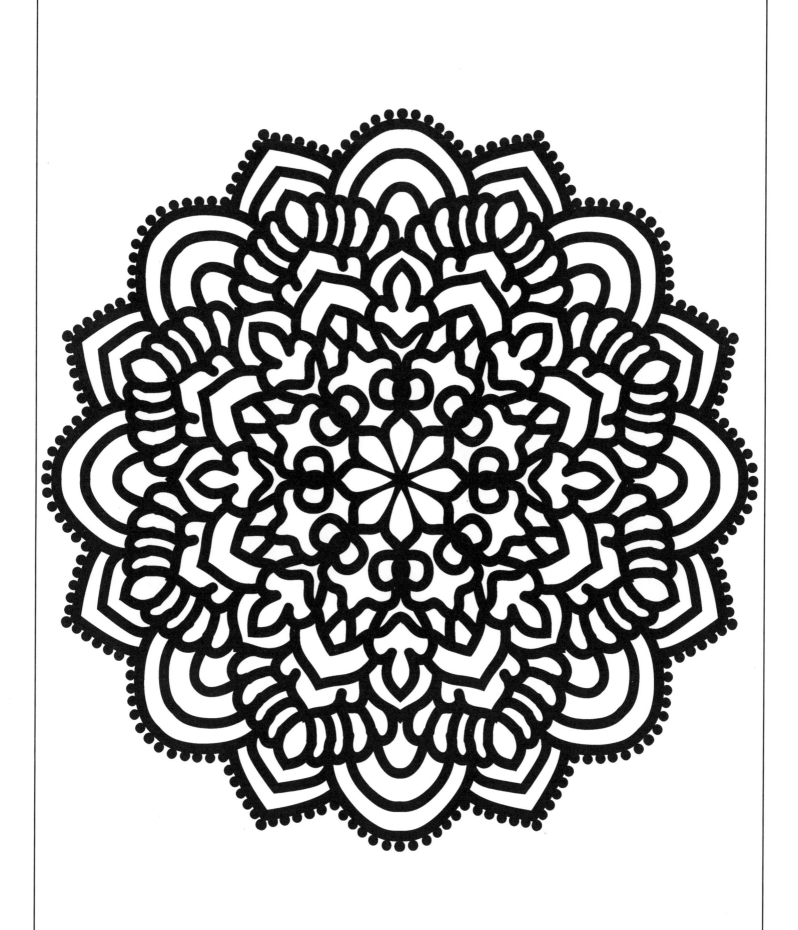

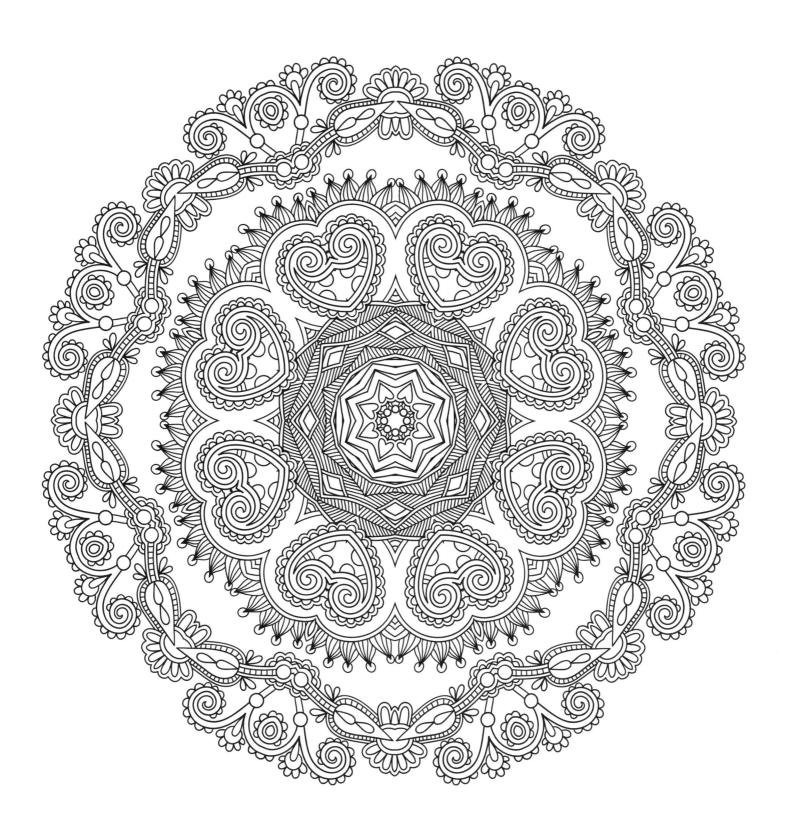

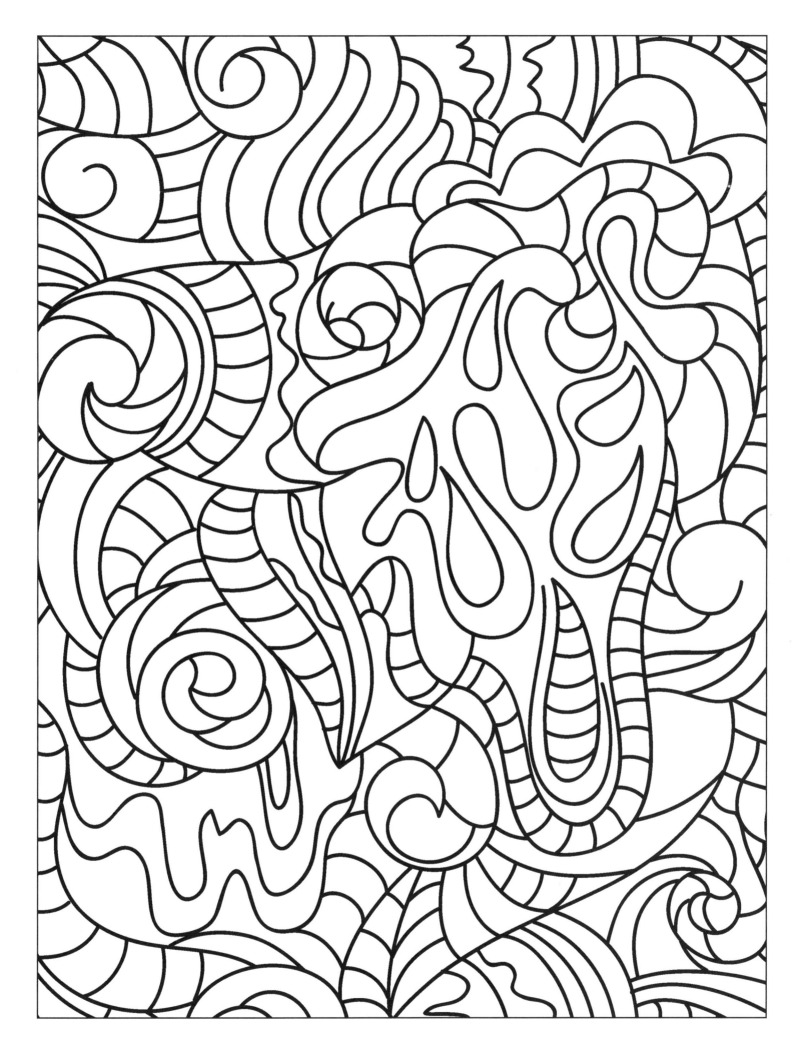

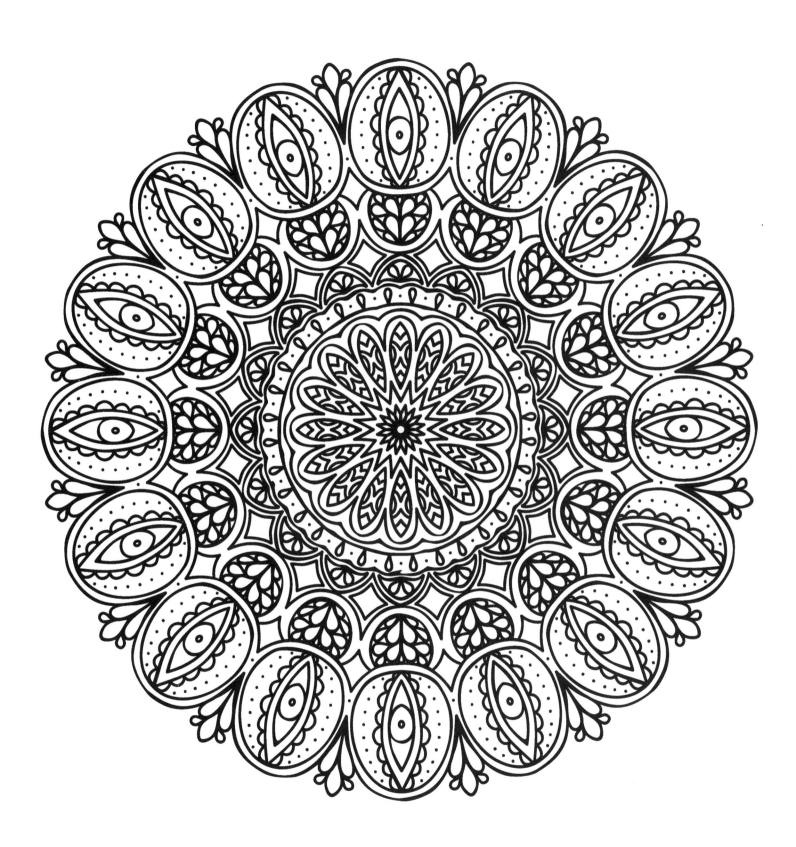

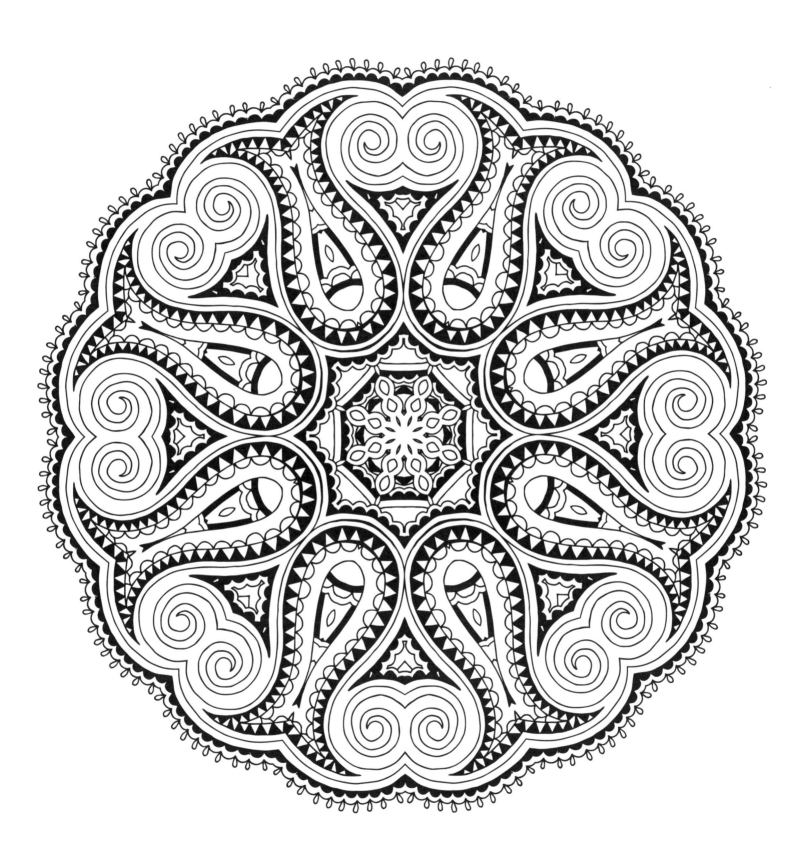

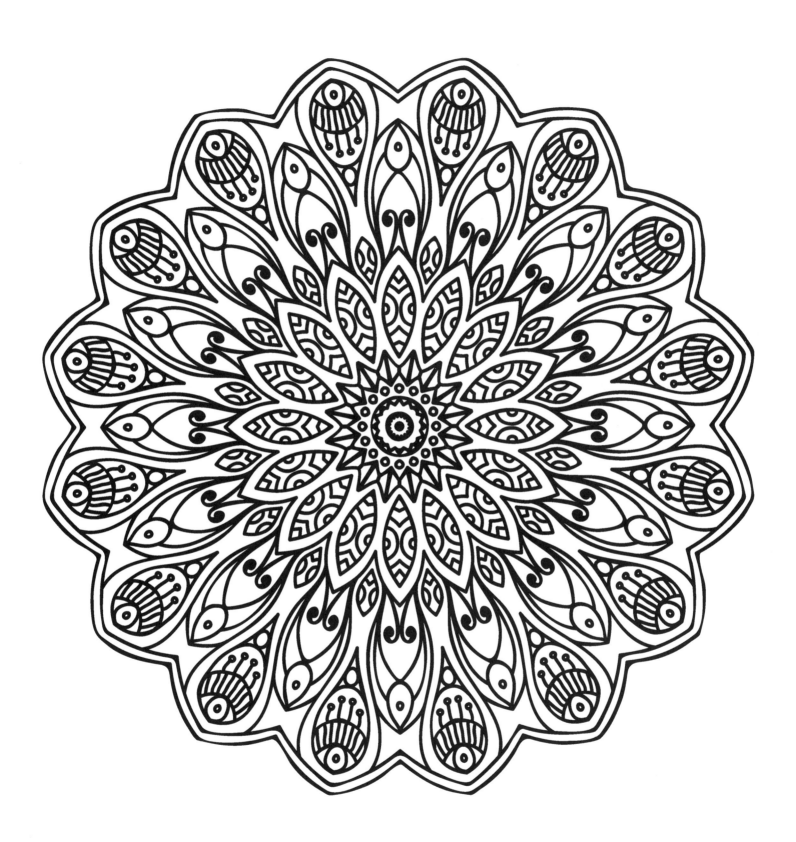

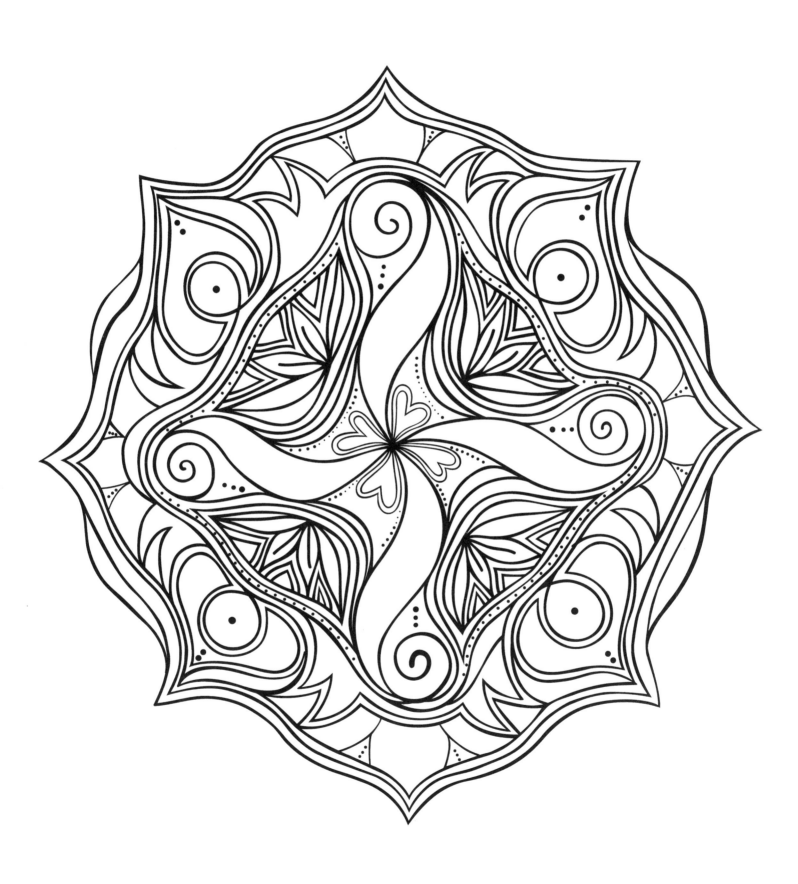

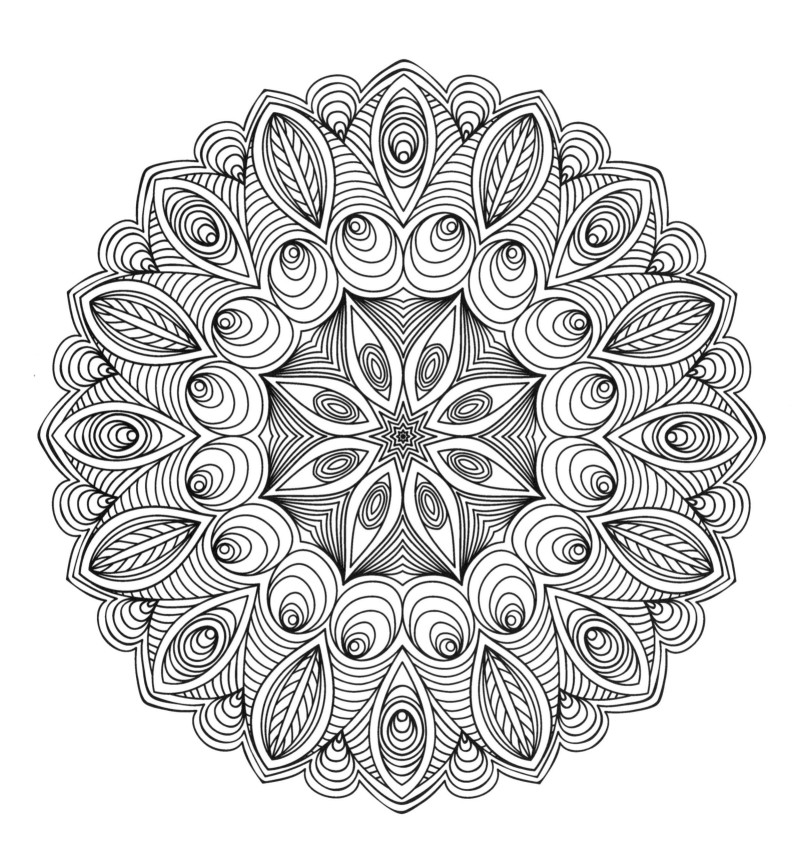

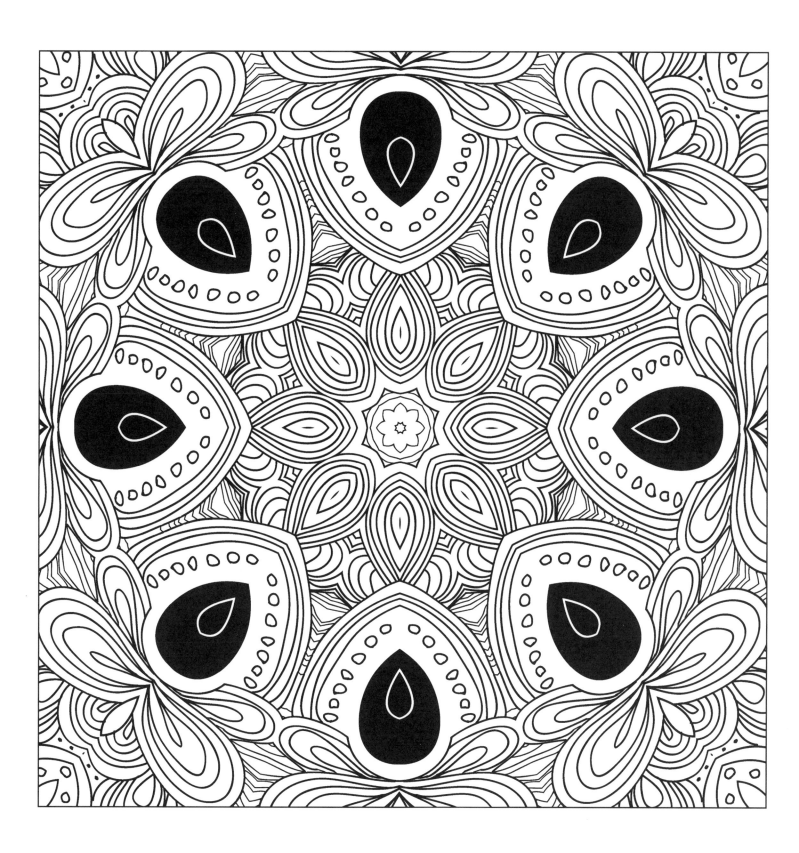

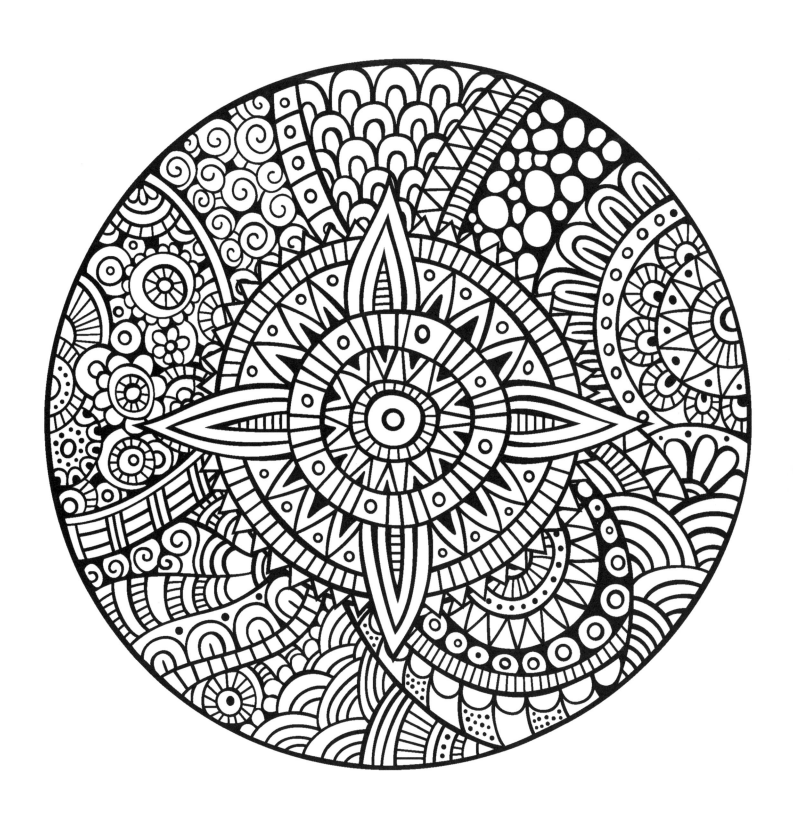

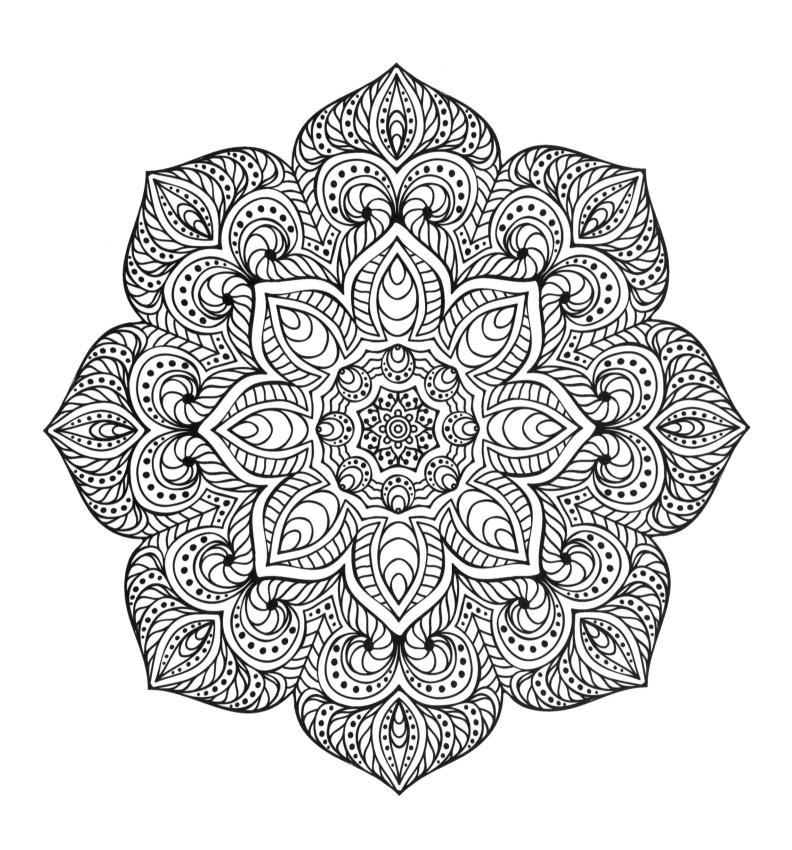

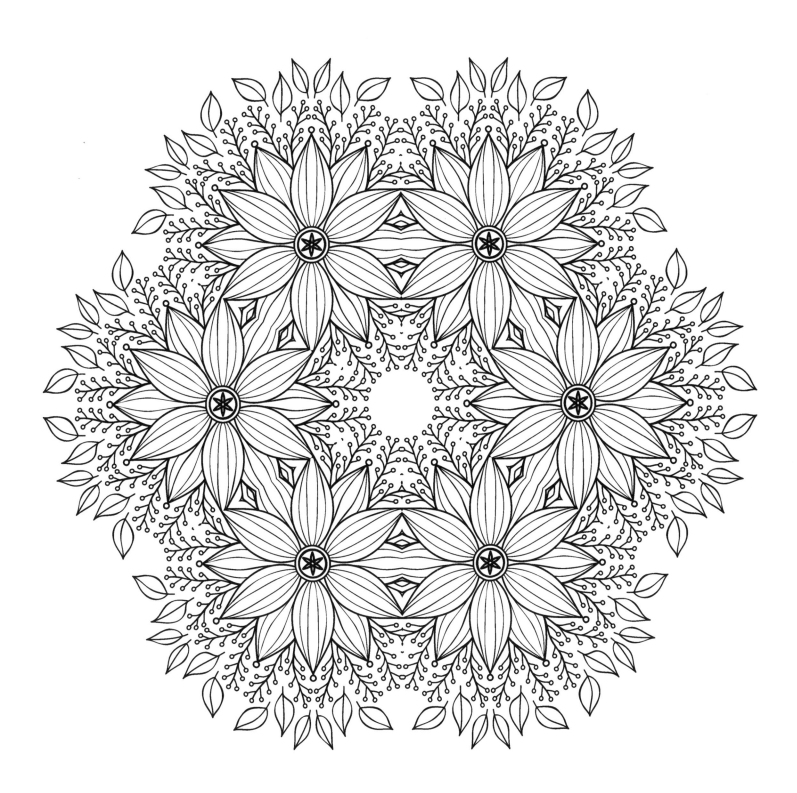

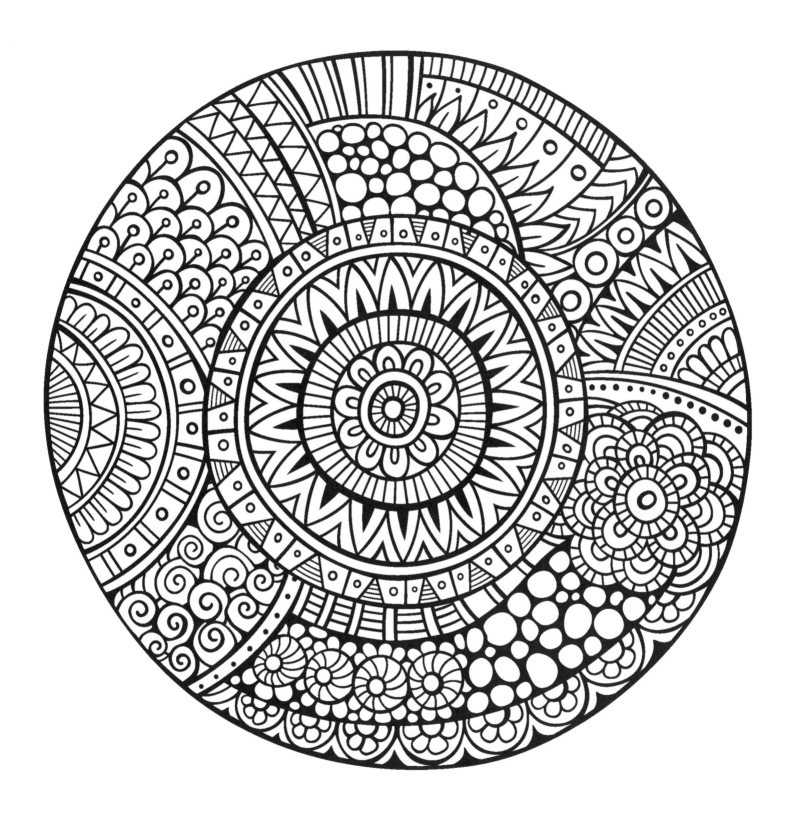

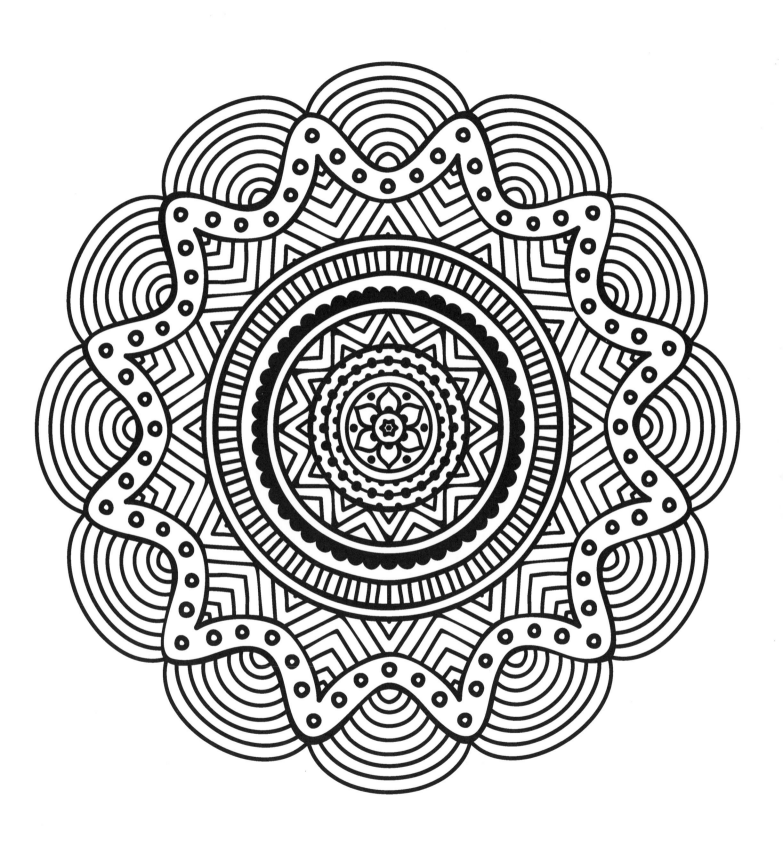